ROBERT HUGH BENSON

CONFESSIONS OF A CONVERT

Fisher Press

Published by Fisher Press, Post Office 41,
Sevenoaks, Kent TN15 6YN, England.

Confessions of a Convert was first published in 1913.
First issued as a Fisher Press paperback 1991.

Line drawings copyright © Mary Tyler 1991.

British Library Cataloguing in Publication Data

A catalogue record for this book is available from
The British Library

ISBN 1 874037 00 0

Set by Computer Techniques, Kemsing, Kent
Printed by Antony Rowe Ltd. Chippenham, Wiltshire
Cover: Brown Knight & Truscott, Tunbridge Wells, Kent

Fisher Press

CONFESSIONS OF A CONVERT

Robert Hugh Benson was born in 1871 at Wellington College, where his father, Edward White Benson, was Headmaster. He was the younger brother of A C and E F Benson, who were also prolific writers. Their father became Archbishop of Canterbury in 1882. Robert Hugh was educated as a scholar at Eton, then at Trinity College, Cambridge. To please his father he took Anglican orders in 1894. His first appointment was with the Eton mission in Hackney Wick. When his father died on his knees at prayer at Hawarden church while visiting Mr Gladstone, Benson read the Litany at the funeral in Canterbury Cathedral.

He was curate at Kemsing, Kent in 1896-7, then, in search of a monastic ideal, joined the Community of the Resurrection at Mirfield. Here he commenced writing seriously. But doubts about the doctrine, discipline and nature of the Anglican Church, began to trouble him. As the son of an Archbishop of Canterbury, his reception into the Catholic Church at the Dominican Priory at Woodchester in 1903 caused a national sensation. After a short period of study in Rome he became a priest of the Catholic Church in 1904. The rest of his short life was devoted to preaching and writing. After volunteering to go to the front as a military chaplain, he died of a pneumonia in 1914, a few weeks after the start of the First World War.

His first book, *The Light Invisible*, a collection of mystical tales, was published in 1903. Fifteen novels, several collections of stories, a book of poems, devotional writing and apologetics, sermons and essays, and several plays for children, followed in rapid succession. His five historical novels are set in Tudor or Stuart England: *By What Authority?* (1904), *The King's Achievement* (1905), *The Queen's Tragedy* (1906), *Come Rack! Come Rope!* (1912), and *Oddsfish!* (1914). *Richard Raynal: Solitary*, his pastiche account of the life of a fifteenth century hermit, was published in 1906. The emotional, religious and moral dilemmas of men and women of Edwardian society are vividly portrayed in *The Sentimentalists* (1906), *The Conventionalists* (1907) *The Necromancers* (1909), *A Winnowing* (1910), *The Coward* (1912), *An Average Man* (1913), *Initiation* (1913), and *Loneliness* (1915). He also wrote two apocalyptic novels, *Lord of the World* (1907) and *The Dawn of All* (1911) about the future of European civilisation and Christendom, which foreshadow aspects of Huxley's *Brave New World* and Orwell's *1984*.

Acknowledgement

We are grateful to Mr Victor Bowden, the owner of the watercolour of St Mary's Church, Kemsing by J S Morland, for permission to use it as part of the design for the cover of this book. Benson was curate at St Mary's in 1897 when the Rev Thomas Carleton Skarratt was vicar. Skarratt's considerable refinement and Anglo-Cathoic views undoubtedly encouraged Benson to come to this tiny village for his curacy. The reredos, canopy and east window in the Gothic style, as depicted on the cover, were all designed by Sir Ninian Comper at Skarratt's behest.

Publisher's note

As the author makes clear in the Preface, this work was first published as a series of articles in an American magazine. The text of this edition includes Benson's corrections and additions for the 1913 edition. Since the revision for book format appears not to have been complete, a few further changes have been made to the layout of the paragraphs.

PREFACE
TO THE FIRST EDITION

THE following chapters were first published, in substance, in the American Catholic magazine, *The Ave Maria*, in 1906-1907, and it is by kind permission of the Editor, Father Hudson, that they are now reprinted, with a few additions and corrections.

During the time that has elapsed since their serial appearance, the writer has received a very large number of applications that they should be issued in book form; and after long hesitation, he has acceded to these requests. He hesitated partly because it appeared to him really doubtful whether their issue would be of any real service at all, partly because he occasionally contemplated adding considerably to them, and annexing to them further "confessions of a convert" since his conversion. This latter idea, however, he has abandoned for the present, owing to the extraordinary difficulty he has found in drawing any real comparison between the rapidly fading impression of Anglicanism upon his memory, and the continually deepening experience of the Catholic religion.

Cardinal Newman compares, somewhere, the sensations of a convert from Anglicanism to those of a man in a fairy story, who, after wandering all night in a city of enchantment, turns after sunrise to look back upon it, and finds to his astonishment that the buildings are no longer there; they have gone up like wraiths and mists under the light of the risen day.

So the present writer has found. He no longer, as in the first months of his conversion, is capable of comparing the two systems of belief together, since that which he has left appears to him no longer a coherent system at all. There are, of course, associations, memories and emotions still left in his mind— some of them very sacred and dear to his heart; he still is happy in numbering among his friends many persons who still find amongst those associations and memories a system which they believe to be the religion instituted by Jesus Christ; yet he himself can no longer see in them anything more than hints and fragments and aspirations detached from the centre and reconstructed into a purely human edifice without foundation and solidity.

Yet he is conscious of no bitterness at all— at the worst he experiences sometimes a touch of impatience merely at the thought of having delayed so long by the shadows from the possession of the divine substance. He cannot, however, with justice, compare the two systems at all; one cannot compare a dream with a reality.

He has abandoned, therefore, the attempt— which lack of leisure in any case would make practically useless— to place side by side with his drowsy memories of Anglicanism the story of his vivid adventures under the sunlight of Eternal Truth. And he publishes the history of the long-drawn process whereby he passed from the one to the other, purely on the advice of numerous friends and inquirers. He is conscious of the appalling egotism of such pages as these; yet he has still to learn how an autobiography can be written without it.

ROBERT HUGH BENSON - Edinburgh, November 1912.

Lincoln Cathedral

CHAPTER ONE

WHEN one stands at last upon high ground, it is extraordinarily difficult to trace the road behind by which one has approached: it winds, rises, falls, broadens, and narrows, until the mind is bewildered. Nor indeed do the comments of friends and critics shouted from below tend to clear the situation.

I have been told that I became a Catholic because I was dispirited at failure and because I was elated at success; because I was imaginative and because I was unperceptive; because I was not hopeful enough and because I was too hopeful, faithless and too trusting, too ardent and too despairing, proud and pusillanimous. I have even been told, since the first publication of these papers, that I have never truly understood the Church of England. Of course that is possible; but, if so, it is certainly not for lack of opportunity.

I was brought up, as will be seen presently, in an ecclesiastical household for twenty-five years; I was a clergyman for nine years, in town and country and a Religious House. My father was the spiritual head of the Anglican communion; my mother, brothers, and sister are still members of it, as well as a large number of my friends. I was prepared for orders by the most eminent Evangelical of his day. I ended by becoming a convinced High Churchman. It seems, further, now that I have my pen in my hand, that I never before really attempted to disentangle the strands, and that it is rash of me to attempt it now. It is full of danger.

It is extremely easy to deceive oneself, and it is extremely hard not to be self-conscious and complacent, not to see only what one would wish to see; and, above everything, one is afraid that, after all, it is bound to be very unconvincing to other people. For you cannot trace the guidance of the Spirit of God or diagnose His operations in the secret rooms of the soul: He seems at times to let good go and to bring instead good out of evil, and light into voluntary darkness...

At the best, therefore, all that is possible is to describe the external features of the country through which the soul has passed—the crossroads, the obstacles, the ravines—and to give some sort of account of the consultations held by the way. Faith, after all, is a divine operation wrought in the dark, even though it may seem to be embodied in intellectual arguments and historical facts; for it is necessary to remember that two equally sincere and intelligent souls may encounter the same external evidences and draw mutually exclusive conclusions from them. The real heart of the matter lies somewhere else... Catechumens, therefore, must remember that while on the one side they must of course clear the ground by the action of the intellect, on the other side it is far more vital that they should pray, purify motives, and yield themselves to God.

First, I think, it will be as well to describe, so far as is possible, my original religious education and position.

I was brought up in the moderate High Church school of thought, and naturally accepted that position as the one most truly representative of the

Anglican communion. I learned—that is to say, so far as I could understand them—the tenets of the Caroline divines; I was taught to be reverent, sober-minded, anti-Roman; to believe in the Real Presence without defining it; to appreciate stateliness, dignity, and beauty in worship; to study first the Bible in general and later the Greek Testament. It seems to me, if I may say it without impertinence, that my religious education was excellently wise.

I was interested in religion; I worshipped in dignified cathedrals and churches; I was allowed to go out before the sermon; I was told the stories of Dr. Neale and the allegories of Dr. Wilberforce and the histories of the early Christian martyrs; and the virtues held up to me as the most admirable were those of truthfulness, courage, honour, obedience, and reverence. I do not think that I loved God consciously, but at least I was never frightened at the presentation of Him or terrified by the threat of hell. I think I accepted Him quite unemotionally as a universal Parental Presence and Authority. The Person of Our Lord I apprehended more from the Gospels than from spiritual experience; I thought of Him in the past and the future tenses, seldom in the present.

My father's influence upon me was always so great that I despair of describing it. I do not think that he understood me very well; but his personality was so dominant and insistent that the lack of this understanding made very little difference; he formed and moulded my views on religious matters in such a manner that it would have seemed to me, while he lived, a kind of blasphemy to have held other opinions than his. Certain points in his system of belief puzzled me then, and they puzzle me still; yet these no more produced in my mind any serious question as to the soundness and truth of his faith than intellectual difficulties in God's Revelation produce doubts in my mind at the present time.

He was, in the main, a High Churchman of the old school; he had an intense love of dignity and splendour in divine worship, a great sense of Church authority, and a firm orthodoxy with regard to the main foundations of the Christian Creed. Yet while he would say, partly humorously, yet with a great deal of seriousness too, that he ought really to have been a canon in a French cathedral, while he would recite scrupulously every day the morning and evening prayer of the Church of England, while he had an intense love of Church history and a deep knowledge both of that and of Christian liturgies and the writings of the Fathers, yet, in quite unexpected points he would fail, as it seemed to me, in carrying out his principles.

For example, there is no custom more deeply rooted in antiquity or more explicitly enjoined in the Book of Common Prayer than that of the Friday fast; there is scarcely any ecclesiastical discipline more primitive than that which forbids the marriage of a man who has already received Major Orders; there is nothing more clear, I should have thought, among the disputed questions of matrimony, than that the release of one partner, with leave to marry again, simultaneously releases the other partner from the bond. Yet I am still wholly unable to understand, remembering his enthusiastic love of what I may call Church principles, how my father justified—as I am convinced he did justify—his attitude to those three points. For I never remember his abstaining from meat on a Friday or any other day, though I know that he denied himself instead in other ways; he raised no objections, except on purely private grounds, to Anglican clergy or bishops contracting marriage; and he held, I know, that while the guilty party, when a divorce had been pronounced by the law of the land, must not seek the blessing of the Church upon a subsequent union, the "innocent party" was perfectly at liberty to do so.

Again, I never understood, and do not understand now, how my father interpreted the words "I believe in the Holy Catholic Church." He would rule out, I know, from external unity those bodies of Christians that do not even claim to possess episcopal succession; he hesitated, as I shall relate presently, as to whether or no the Church of Rome had forfeited, through her profession of what he believed to be heretical doctrines, her place in the body of Christ; yet he showed the greatest sympathy with and care for certain groups of Eastern Christians whose tenets have been explicitly condemned by Councils which he himself would acknowledge as ecumenical.

Again, I have never really understood his attitude towards such doctrines as those of the Sacrament of Penance. He held firmly in theory that Jesus Christ has given authority to His ministers to "declare and pronounce to his people, being penitent, the absolution and remission of their sins"; and, as a matter of practice, he himself, at a certain crisis in my life, recommended to me, when I told him that I wished to go to Confession, a "discreet and learned" clergyman to whom I had better apply; yet he never urged the practice, so far as I am aware, upon anyone, and never went to Confession himself.

He believed, then, in the Power of the Keys; yet he seemed to hold simultaneously that this relief was to be sought only if peace of mind could not be obtained by other means, unless, indeed, he held, as I think possible, that the Power was effectively exercised in the public "absolutions" uttered in the course of the Church services. He appears, therefore, on the surface, to have held that the authority given with such extraordinary solemnity by Christ to His Apostles, was not in the least even normally necessary to the forgiveness of post-baptismal mortal sin.

Now I am perfectly convinced that my father did not believe himself inconsistent—that he had, in fact, principles which reconciled to his own mind these apparent contradictions. Yet I never knew, and do not now know, what they were. For, though he loved nothing better than to be consulted by his children on religious matters, as a matter of fact he was not very approachable by timid minds. I used always to be a little afraid of showing ignorance, and still more of shocking him. Never once, in a genuine difficulty, did I find him anything but utterly tender and considerate; yet his intense personality and his almost fierce faith continually produced in me the vision that he would think it unfilial for me to do anything except acquiesce instantly in his judgment; the result was that I was often completely at a loss as to what that judgment was.

Religion at home, then, was always coloured and vivified by my father's individuality. I remember even now the sense of finality and completeness which it conveyed. The morning and evening services, first in the tiny prayer room at Lincoln, where my father was Chancellor from my first to my fifth year, then in the beautiful minute chapel at Lis Escop, Truro, where he was Bishop until after my thirteenth birthday, and finally in the lovely chapels at Lambeth and Addington after his elevation to the see of Canterbury—these services, every detail of which was thought out by my father and carried out liturgically and reverently, still have a strange aroma to my mind that I suppose my memory will never lose.

Other ways in which my father influenced my religion were as follows.

On Sunday afternoons in the country we would walk with him, rather slowly and recollectedly, for about an hour and a half; and during these expeditions one of us would usually read aloud, or some times my father himself would read aloud from some religious book. I do not think that these books were very well selected for a boy's point of view. The poems of George Herbert were frequently read on these occasions, and these very peculiar, scholarly, and ingenious meditations used to produce in me, occasionally, a sudden thrill of pleasure, but far more commonly a kind of despairing impatience.

Or, again, some interminable life of a saint or a volume of Church history would be read; or a book of Dean Stanley's on the Holy Land. Once only can I remember, with real delight, so far back as early in the eighties, how my father fascinated me for half an hour or so by reading aloud, as we walked, the martyrdom of St. Perpetua and her companions. I remember, too, the irrepressible awe with which I discovered presently that he had been translating aloud and at sight, in perfect English and without hesitation, from the Latin *Acta Martyrum*.

At the close of these Sunday walks, and sometimes also on weekdays after breakfast, we would go to my father's study for Bible-reading or Greek Testament. It is difficult to describe these lessons. For the most part my father would comment continuously and brilliantly, though often far above my capacity to understand, putting questions occasionally, showing great pleasure when we answered intelligently, or, still more, when we put reasonable questions of our own, and a rather oppressive disappointment when we were listless or stupid.

It was all extremely stimulating to the intellect; it was, also, always somewhat of a strain; but I think now that its lack consisted in the predominance of the mind element over the soul. I do not remember that these lessons made it easier to love God; they were often interesting, and sometimes absorbing; but I do not, with all reverence to my father's memory, even now believe that in myself they developed the spiritual side of religion.

For himself, with his own great spirituality, it was natural enough that his soul should find pleasurable activity in the intellectual scholarly plane; for myself there was a considerable tendency to think that intellectualism and Greek Testament ought to be the very heart of religion.

For a child, I believe, there are other moulds more natural than that of the intellect in which spiritual life may shape itself: little pieces of ceremonial, connected, for example, with the saying of his prayers, actions of reverence, such as the sign of the cross or the fingering of beads, symbolic objects of worship, such as crucifixes or statues, and, for instruction, an almost endless use of attractive and well-drawn pictures—these, I believe, are a better machinery for the shaping and development of a child's spiritual life than the methods of the intellect. I remember, for instance, that while George Herbert's poems usually bored and irritated me, I found a real attraction in the quaint devices of "Easter wings" or the "altar"—the outlines, that is to say, in which once or twice he prints his verses on the page.

As regards morality, I was also a little puzzled by my father's attitude. He had a very great sense of the duty of obedience, and this sense, I think, rather overpowering in its sternness, tended to obscure to some extent in my own mind the various grades of objective wrongdoing. Two or three sins stood out to me in my childhood, as supremely wicked—such things as lying, thieving, and cruelty. But beyond these practically all other sins seemed to me about the same; to climb over the wire fences that bounded the drive at Lis Escop by putting one's feet anywhere except at the point where the wire pierced the upright railings —(my father bade me always do this to avoid stretching the wire)—seemed to me about as wicked as to lose my temper, to sulk, or to be guilty of meanness. In this way, to some degree, one's appreciation of morality was, I think, a little dulled: since to forget an order, or to disregard it in a moment of blinding excitement, was visited by my father with what appeared to be as much anger as if it had been a deliberate moral fault.

Once, later, at Eton, I was accused of grave cruelty to another boy and was very nearly flogged for it. I happened to be innocent and, ultimately, cleared myself entirely of the charge after a very searching examination by the head master; but for the time, after the news of the charge had come to my father in the holidays while I was at home, I was very nearly paralysed in mind by the appalling atmosphere of my father's indignation and wholly failed to defend myself except by tears and silent despair. Yet all the time I was conscious of a faint relief in the knowledge that even if I were guilty—and at the time so confused was I that I really scarcely knew whether I were guilty or not— my father could not possibly be angrier with me than he had been, for instance, when I threw stones at the goldfish in the pond or played with my fingers during prayers.

Such, more or less, was my father's influence upon my religious life. I do not, as I have said, think that he made it easy to love God; but he did, undoubtedly, establish in my mind an ineradicable sense of a Moral Government in the universe, of a tremendous Power behind phenomena, of an austere and orderly dignity with which this Moral Power presented itself. He himself was wonderfully tender-hearted and loving, intensely desirous of my good, and, if I had but known it, touchingly covetous of my love and confidence; yet his very anxiety on my behalf to some degree obscured the fire of his love, or, rather, caused it to affect me as heat rather than as light. He dominated me completely by his own forcefulness, and I felt when he died, as a man said to me of his own parallel experience, as if the roof were lifted off the world.

At my private school in Clevedon we attended a church rather more "high" than those to which I had been accustomed. It contained a dark, mystical-looking sanctuary, with iron and brass gates; the clergy wore coloured stoles, and Gregorian chants were in use. But I have not the slightest recollection of being astonished at any difference of doctrine from that which I had learned; though I was, I think, a little awed and curious at the minute variations of ritual, and certainly depressed by the species of plain-song we employed.

At Eton, however, I found myself back again in the familiar academic atmosphere of plain dignity, beautiful singing, and indefiniteness of dogma; and it was here, I suppose, that I should have received deep impressions of religion. But I did not, nor did any other boy of my acquaintance, so far as I am aware.

My Confirmation was postponed a year or two, because I was supposed to be indifferent to it, as indeed I was. I regarded it as a seemly ceremony, to be undergone with gravity, and to represent a kind of spiritual coming of age; and I was really surprised when, upon at last inquiring of my father as to when I was to be confirmed, since most of my friends already were so, I was told that I ought to have been confirmed a year before, but that the rite had been postponed because I had not seemed to desire it. However, since I had taken the initiative at last, it should be as I suggested. I heard this with a faint sense of injustice; for I had become so accustomed to follow my father's lead in matters of religion that it had never even occurred to me that in any matter I ought to take the initiative myself.

But even Confirmation, combined with very loving and impressive talks from my father, made no difference to me. For my preparation I went to "my tutor," who talked to me about half a dozen times alone, chiefly on morality and the need of being strenuous. I cannot remember that much was said about doctrine; it was, rather, taken for granted. For example, a kind of informal confession was suggested to me tentatively, though no word was said of absolution, and indeed the idea of such a thing was completely unfamiliar to me. I answered that I had nothing I wished to reveal. Finally, Dr. Goulburn's *Personal Religion*, a stout, unattractive book, was presented to me. A year or two ago I found it again, and noticed that the leaves were still uncut. So little impression, in fact, did the whole affair make on me that I cannot remember even what Bishop it was that performed the ceremony; though I think it must have been the famous historian, Dr. Stubbs, of Oxford.

The only incident connected with my confirmation that is really clear to my mind is an anxious consultation held afterwards with three friends as to whether it would be decent to play fives in the afternoon, or whether it would be more proper to spend the time in decorous silence. We were not, I believe, in the least hypocritical or contemptuous; we wished to do what was right in the matter; and if fives could be reconciled with it, so much the better. We decided to play, and did so with a slightly chastened air. My mother also, soon after, gave me a little silver Maltese cross, engraved with the date of my confirmation—March 26, 1887. I wore it on my watch chain for a while—for at Eton at that time there was as little opposition as enthusiasm towards religion— and presently lost it.

On the day of Communion I think I was rather more impressed. It was all unusual and mysterious; for only once before in my life had I even attended the service. I vaguely believed that I entered into a closer relationship with my Divine Ruler than ever before; and, although I was slightly depressed at the thought that in future I must behave myself better, I believed that I sincerely intended to do so.

Two other incidents I also remember connected with religion about this time. The first was my discovery, in a deserted tower-room at Lambeth, of a copy of Dr. Ken's *Prayers for Winchester Scholars*, which somehow appealed to my imagination, and in which my father with great pleasure wrote my name when I asked him if I might have the book. I used this assiduously for a few months, liking, I think, the English and a certain gracious formality about the book. Then I dropped my prayers altogether and only went to Communion—though each time, I think, with tolerably good intentions— so often as it was necessary to avoid attention.

The second incident was one entirely uncharacteristic of Eton. The son of an Evangelical dignitary underwent some sort of a religious crisis at home and set to work with praiseworthy zeal upon his acquaintances. I was one of them, and was persuaded by him, with a friend of mine, to attend a Bible-reading, with prayer, held in his room. About four other boys assembled, and we sat there in horror, exchanging furtive glances while our leader expounded. At the sound of a footstep outside, Bibles vanished as if in conjuring tricks, and the exercises, I remember, were brought to an end after two meetings by a sudden irrepressible explosion of laughter from my own particular friend. He sat there, scarlet-faced, with the tears streaming down his cheeks and laughter bursting from him in successive explosions, while the rest of us giggled and eyed our instructor alternately. I think that the whole affair would have been extremely unhealthy if it had affected us in the slightest. Fortunately it did not, and we came away with our opinion unchanged that such zeal was all rather "bad form" and of no value.

Our evangeliser, however, was not discouraged, and his next attempt was more serious. He managed somehow to persuade an "old boy" to come down to Eton and address the house, which he did, I regret to say, in the presence of the house-master. It was very terrible. He delivered an emotional speech that was practically an open confession of his own evil living at school. I do not think I have ever seen boys more sincerely horrified—not indeed at the substance of his story, but at the appalling "bad form" of alluding to it in a public manner.

This same attitude towards morality manifested itself in other ways. Chapel services at Eton counted for very little indeed usually in a religious direction; they were rather artistic, very academic, and represented, I think, the same kind of official homage to Almighty God as cheering the Queen when she came to see us, or when we, as on the occasion of her first Jubilee, went to the Castle to see her, represented our loyalty towards Victoria. You might or might not be personally enthusiastic, but at least you must pay a seemly deference.

Now and again, however, one clerical master in particular would make an honest attempt to appeal personally in a sermon to the consciences of his hearers, especially on the subject of purity. Now his hearers, in the main, had no common code on the matter at all. A boy might be fantastically evil in that regard or scrupulously fastidious, without in the least forfeiting the respect of his fellows; it was, according to the Eton code of that time, simply a matter of personal taste. Some things you must not be: you must not be personally dirty, or a coward, or a bully, or a thief; but in this other matter you could choose for yourself without being thought either a blackguard or a prude, if you made the one choice, or if you made the other.

These appeals, therefore, from the pulpit, made usually with a great deal of sincere ardour, were merely looked upon as slightly absurd. The authorities had their view on the subject, of course—we knew that—and we had the other. No kind of impression, therefore, was ever made by these fervent discourses—since the preacher was nothing of a real orator—and no comment ever uttered upon them except an observation, perhaps, that "A seemed very excited to-day." In a word, such warmth of feeling upon a subject on which our minds were completely made up, one way or the other, seemed to us to be slightly bad form. In any case, too, it was not a subject for public discussion.

It was the lack of individual dealing with the soul, then, that was accountable for so much evil. Efforts have been recently made, I believe, to remedy this in some degree; and yet the true and only remedy is, as a matter of fact, practically impossible. Until something resembling the business-like system of Catholic schools in the encouragement of private devotion, the regularity of Confession, or at least the recognition of some such practice as a reasonable mode of relief—until these things in some form or another find their places in the great Protestant public schools, I do not understand how the public formalities of religion can be anything more than formalities. And yet nothing but the peculiar safeguards of the Catholic Confessional can really meet the case, and these, from the very nature of the case, are out of the question. A purely voluntary system of Confession, such as they practised at the Woodard schools, though better than nothing, yet has unavoidable drawbacks.

It was after leaving Eton, and before going up to Cambridge, that I received what was really the first touch of personal religion. I was in London for a year or so, and for a short time I was vaguely interested by Theosophy; then suddenly I became entirely absorbed and fascinated by the music and dignity of worship in St. Paul's Cathedral. The high celebration there is, indeed, as Gounod is supposed to have said, one of the most impressive religious functions in Europe. I began to go to Communion every week and to attend every other service that I could possibly manage—sometimes in the organ loft, watching the mysteries of the keys and stops, sometimes sitting in the stalls. I did not in the least appreciate the sermons, though I was vaguely affected by Canon Liddon.

It was the music, first and last, and it was through that opening that I first began to catch glimpses of the spiritual world; and my sense of worship was further developed and directed by an absolute passion that I conceived for Mr. Shorthouse's book, *John Inglesant*. I read it again and again, as I read it still, though aware of its tendency to Pantheism; and even now I know passages of it by heart, particularly those dealing with the Person of Our Lord. It seemed that I had found at last the secret of those vague religious ceremonies to which I had always conformed with uninterested equanimity. A very warm friendship or two, also formed at this time, helped me in the same direction.

At Cambridge everything receded once more, with the exception of a sudden short and intense interest in Swedenborgianism. Then I lost all interest. I neglected my prayers, except for a while when my father gave me a beautiful edition of Bishop Andrews' *Preces Privatæ* in Greek and Latin; I almost gave up Communion; and the sole thread that was left to attach me in any sense to the supernatural was, once more, music. I very seldom attended my own chapel, but went instead continually to the evening service at King's, which, in another way from that of St. Paul's Cathedral, was, and is, quite incomparable.

About half a dozen times, too, I attended—with a recent convert, also an old Etonian—High Mass at the Catholic church, where I worked later as a priest; but it made no impression on me, except one of vaguely mingled contempt and awe. But I remember distinctly an agreeable sense of shock and elation when at the Asperges one day I felt a drop of holy water on my face. My friend lent to me a *Garden of the Soul*, which I never returned to him. Twelve years later, when I was myself a Catholic, I wrote to remind him of this, observing that now the book was more mine than ever.

Of course what religion I had was very little more

than artistic; it made no sort of difference to my actions, but it kept me just in touch with things that were not wholly of this world. My relations with regard to religion are very aptly illustrated by a little adventure I passed through in Switzerland about this time.

One of my brothers and I were ascending the Piz Palu, a peak of the Bernina range in the Engadine, and upon reaching the summit after a very laborious climb from a little after midnight until eight o'clock in the morning through very heavy snow, my heart suddenly collapsed. I was dosed with neat brandy, but owing to very severe training recently undergone at Cambridge to reduce my steering weight, this failed properly to restore me, and for about two hours I was carried along the arête of the mountain apparently unconscious: my brother, indeed, for the greater part of that time thought me actually dead. Now although I appeared unconscious, and for a while was so, I was perfectly aware, even when my senses failed to act, that I was dying; I even began to speculate what would be the first phenomenon of the supernatural world that would disclose itself to me; and I fancied, owing no doubt to the suggestion conveyed to me by the vast icy peaks on which I had closed my eyes, that this would be a vision of the Great White Throne.

Yet never for one instant was I conscious of the least touch of apprehensiveness at the thought of meeting God, nor of the least impulse to make an act of contrition for my past life. My religion, such as it was, was of so impersonal and unvital a nature that, while I never doubted the objective truth of what I had been taught, I neither feared God nor loved Him: I felt no sense of responsibility towards Him, nor was I even moved at the prospect of seeing Him. I acquiesced passively in my belief that He was present, but neither shrank from Him in fear nor aspired towards Him with affection.

And this I think, was typical of my whole attitude towards religion in ordinary life. Intellectually I accepted the Christian Creed; scarcely at all with my will or my emotion. Except in moments, or for short periods of superficial excitement I was wholly uninterested. My religion had no spark in it of real vitality.

In fact, my closest friend at this time was an explicitly dogmatic atheist—I think the only one I have met—and I was conscious of no particularly alarming gulf between us. One other friend of mine also was a Catholic, and with him I used to argue sometimes. But I do not think it ever occurred to me as even conceivable that his tenets could be anything but obviously absurd, though I remember being extremely annoyed one day when my atheist friend, being appealed to as an arbitrator, declared that, granted Christianity, Catholicism was its only possible interpretation. For the most part, however, I was really indifferent, spending a good deal of time in hypnotism in which I was tolerably proficient. No person in authority ever, so far as I can remember, made the slightest effort to approach me on matters of religion.

And then—even to this day I do not know why—I decided to become a clergyman. I think the death of one of my sisters about this time helped me to the decision. But, for the rest, I suspect that my motives rose largely from the fact that a clerical life seemed to me to offer the line of least resistance. I am sure that I was not calculating enough to argue to myself that being my father's son would bring me emoluments or promotion; for, honestly, these were no temptation to me at all; but I think that, on the natural side at any rate, a life spent in an ecclesiastical household, and the absence of any other particular interest, seemed to indicate the following of my father's profession as, on the whole, the simplest solution of the problems of my future. I knew, too, that my decision would give him extraordinary pleasure, and I valued his approval very highly indeed.

But I think I was fairly conscientious about it all. I still had, from time to time, romantic experiences in spiritual matters and loved, spasmodically and sentimentally, or thought I loved, the Person of Our Divine Lord, as suggested to me by *John Inglesant*; and I intended, sincerely enough, to embrace the clerical life with my heart and will, and to live it as little unworthily as possible. These intentions too were, as I have said, clinched and brought to a point by the very keen emotions I experienced at the death of my sister, and by a little message she sent to me from her death bed.

Things were changed a little then; I began to read theology and became interested in it, especially in dogma, such as it was, and Church history. But it did not even enter my head for an instant that there was anything but the Church of England to represent Christ's original institution. I did not in the least hold, as I tried to hold later, that the Anglican communion was the "Catholic Church" in England, and the Roman communion the Church of the Continent. In fact I remember once in Switzerland remonstrating with a High Church lady who held such views and acted upon them by hearing Mass in a Catholic chapel. The Roman Catholics, I thought, were obviously corrupt and decayed, the Ritualists were tainted, and the extreme Protestants were noisy, extravagant, and vulgar. Plainly there was only one religious life possible, that of a quiet country clergyman, with a beautiful garden, an exquisite choir, and a sober bachelor existence. Marriage seemed to me then, as always, quite inconceivable.

I read for Orders for a year and a half with Dean Vaughan at Llandaff. He was a unique and exceptional man, and it was owing no doubt to his extraordinary charm of personality and his high spirituality that my father, in spite of the divergence of his views from those of the Dean, decided to place me under his charge. I think that he was in some respects the most remarkable preacher I have ever heard. He wrote out his sermons with infinite pains, word for word, destroying, I believe, the entire manuscript and beginning it all over again if he were interrupted during his composition of it; and then delivering it word for word from his paper with scarcely a gesture except quick, slight glances and almost timid movements of his head. But the English was simply perfect, comparable only, I think, to that of Ruskin and Newman; his voice was as smooth and pointed and pliable as the blade of a rapier; and above all, he possessed that magnetic kind of personality that affected his educated hearers, at any rate, like a strain of music.

He was a pronounced Evangelical in his views: I still possess somewhere a couple of sets of notes that I wrote for him, under his influence, on the sacraments of Baptism and the Lord's Supper, in which anything approaching to sacramental doctrine is explicitly denied. Yet his faith was so radiantly strong, his love of the Person of our Lord so intense, that his pupils, I think, whatever their predispositions, were almost unconscious of the lack of other things. When we were under his spell it appeared as if no more could be necessary than the love and devotion of our master to God.

His wife too, a sister of Dean Stanley, was another great feature in our life. She was a strange old lady, resembling in face Queen Victoria, and one of the cleverest women I have ever met. She talked and wrote letters brilliantly and wittily, and it was a real delight to be in her company. When three or four of us were bidden to dinner at the Deanery, we used to compare our notes of invitation in order to triumph in her variety of expression. Each note was quite different from all the rest, yet each was vivid.

I remember the Dean's gentle pleasure when he discovered that, during a grave illness of his, his wife had, in despair of his recovery, actually engaged a house to retire to for her widowhood. He told us the facts in her presence, while she jerked her features about in humorous protest. "No, my dear," said the Dean at last, with his eyes twinkling like stars, "you see I'm not dead yet, after all, and I'm afraid you won't get to your new house just yet."

We led a very harmless life, reading Greek Testament with the Dean every morning, composing a sermon for him once a week, playing a great deal of football, and attending the cathedral services every day. It was one of the proudest days of my life when I was selected by a club to play half-back against Cardiff. But here, in spite of the Dean's strong Evangelicalism, commended though it was by his charming and spiritual personality, I began to have a glimmer of more Catholic views, and, for the first time in my life, began to prefer Communion before breakfast. This was partly through the influence of a particular man with whom I made great friends. *John Inglesant* also began again to reassert his power, and I even made a journey or two here and there to see houses where I might set up, I imagined, an institution resembling that of Nicholas Ferrar at Little Gidding, where, however, women were to be strictly excluded. We were to lead a very recondite life, I remember, in a kind of scholarly solitude; but I do not remember that self-denial in any form was to play a part in it. Yet the intention was certainly good, for the chief object of the life, so far as I contemplated it, was to increase the union of our souls with the Person of Our Blessed Lord.

I was ordained deacon in 1894, after a very strange, solitary retreat, in which for about a week all religious sense deserted me. My retreat was made near Lincoln, where years ago I had lived as a child. I engaged a couple of rooms in the lodge of an old park about four or five miles out of the city and arranged my day in what I thought a suitable manner, giving certain hours to prayer and meditation, to the recitation of the Little Hours, in English, and to exercise. Of course it was an impossibly mad thing to do. I was in a state of tense excitement at the prospect of my ordination to the ministry; I knew nothing whatever about my own soul and the dangers of introspection, and still less about the science of prayer.

The result was such mental agony as I cannot even now remember without an ache of mind. It seemed to me, after a day or two, that there was no truth in religion, that Jesus Christ was not God, that the whole of life was an empty sham, and that I was, if not the chiefest of sinners, at any rate the most monumental of fools. I still remember the torment of Advent Sunday. I walked in the dark of the morning, fasting, into Lincoln, went to Communion in the Cathedral, and attended the services later in the day, sitting in the dusky nave, like a soul in hell. I still cannot read the magnificent collect for Advent Sunday, as appointed in *The Book of Common Prayer*—the rolling phrases about the "works of darkness" and the "armour of light,"—or the tramping hymn, "Lo! He comes with clouds descending," without an echo of the horror coming back to me.

It was on this day that for the first time I set eyes on Bishop King— even then a bent old man with a wonderfully spiritual face, walking swiftly and swayingly at the end of the procession—the Bishop who had recently been tried in my father's Court at Lambeth on charges of Ritualism.

Matters got a little better with me towards the end of my retreat; a kind of dull luminousness of faith came

back, and at last I went back to Addington for my
ordination to the diaconate, though still shaken and,
so to speak, still spiritually hysterical.

The ordination itself distracted and helped me. It
was held by my father in Croydon parish church. I was
selected as "Gospeller"; and Canon Mason, the late
master of Pembroke College, Cambridge, preached an
exceedingly fine and enkindling sermon. I remember
one extremely subtle and witty sentence of it. He was
speaking of the doctrinal divisions in the Church of
England; and, seeking to reassure us on the point,
combined geographical and dogmatic dissension, together with a fine alliterativeness, in one sweeping
phrase. "For all our divisions," he said, "we are yet
united in objective truth. One form of words, and one
only, is being uttered to-day in every diocese—from
Carlisle to Canterbury, from Lincoln to Liverpool."

On the following Christmas Day I assisted my
father in the administration of Communion in
Addington church, and then went at once to work in
East London, at the Eton mission; and here, for the first
time, High Church ideas began to take definite gradual
possession of me. The occasion of it was as follows.

I received an invitation, a month after my ordination, to be present at a retreat at Kemsing, near Sevenoaks, given by one of the Cowley "Fathers." I went, in
high collars and a white tie, and was completely taken
by storm. For the first time Christian Doctrine, as
Father Maturin preached it, displayed itself to me as an
orderly scheme. I saw now how things fitted on one to
the other, how the sacraments followed inevitably
from the Incarnation, how body and spirit were alike
met in the mercy of God.

The preacher was extraordinarily eloquent and
deep; he preached hour after hour; he caught up my
fragments of thought, my glimpses of spiritual experience, my gropings in the twilight, and showed me the

whole, glowing and transfigured in an immense scheme whose existence I had not suspected. He touched my heart also, profoundly, as well as my head, revealing to me the springs and motives of my own nature in a completely new manner. Especially he preached Confession, showing its place in the divine economy; but this, very naturally, I strenuously resisted. It was not a strict retreat, and I talked freely in the afternoon with two friends, endeavouring to persuade myself that Confession was no more than an occasional medicine for those who felt they needed it. But the work was done, though I did not know it until a year later. This, however, I took away, explicit, from the retreat—a desire to make my own that religion which I had heard preached. But there were certain difficulties before me.

The parish to which my father was sending me was not run on at all extreme lines. Confession was distinctly discouraged and the Communion was celebrated on Sundays and Thursdays only. It was an extremely beautiful church, built by Bodley on High Church lines, with Latin inscriptions quite incomprehensible to the congregation. The previous vicar, who had now become Bishop of Zululand, and was a distinct High Churchman, had been recently succeeded by a chaplain of my father's —the Rev. St. Clair Donaldson, now Archbishop of Brisbane, whose views were much more Evangelical.

Mr. Donaldson was a magnificent worker; great men's clubs were in full swing, and activities of every kind—Bands of Hope, Temperance Meetings, a ladies' settlement, children's plays, and, above all, systematic house to house visiting— occupied our time. But the original High Church methods of Bishop Carter had been largely modified, the daily celebration had been abolished, and the Anglican sisters, who had previously worked in the parish, had, thereupon, withdrawn. I believe that the Vicar did occasionally

hear confessions in the vestry from two or three
adherents of the old system, but he certainly neither
preached nor encouraged the practice in any way.

In spite of his influence, however, the ideas sown
in my mind by Father Maturin began to sprout. It
seemed to me then, and it seems to me still, even
looking at it from the Anglican point of view, as if the
only hope of really touching and holding the lives of
those who live under the stress of East London sordid-
ness and pressure, lies in what may be called the
materialisation of religion—I mean the supplying of
acts and images on which religious emotion may
concentrate itself. Extreme definiteness seems necessary, and that, not only in the bright and impressive
adjuncts of worship, but in the modes in which individual approach to God is made.

Men's clubs, where religious and political conversation is against the rules,(as was the case in ours),
furious visiting, children's pantomimes, and general
activity and fervour certainly have their place and
function; but unless the individual understands where
and how he may discharge his penitence or adoration,
not merely as a member of a congregation, but as an
unique soul which God has made and redeemed, piety
can never be more than vague and diffusive. I dimly
felt this, even then, and, since a man's soul is nearer to
himself than any other can be, I began to see that I
must begin with myself.

The end of it was that just before my ordination as
"priest" I made, with my father's consent, for the first
time, a full confession of my whole life before a
clergyman. He was extraordinarily kind and skilful,
though he gave me a penance which would occupy me
half an hour every day until I came to him again,
three months after. And the joy that followed that
confession was simply indescribable. I went home in
a kind of ecstasy.

My ordination also was an immense happiness, though I see now that there was a considerable feverishness in my emotions. I went into the Addington woods alone, telling myself that I was now a priest, that I could do for others what had been recently done for me; and I went back to East London full of enthusiasm.

About this time, too, I began to take up again my acquaintance with the Cambridge friend with whom I had had many arguments—now an Oratorian novice—and went to see him several times; but I do not think it ever seriously entered my head that his intellectual position could possibly be anything but ridiculous. Still, he was a charming man, and, I have no doubt, did much to break down the wall of misunderstanding that separated my mind from his. I was perfectly confident, perfectly content, and perfectly obstinate. So fearless was I of his influence that I even went to stay with him on the coast of Cornwall, and while there, having no cassock of my own, borrowed and, in a sort of joyful excitement, wore his Religious habit in the pulpit of the little parish church.

In October, 1896 my father suddenly died on his knees in church during a visit to Mr. Gladstone at Hawarden. I was superintending the Sunday school at the Eton Mission when a telegram was put into my hands announcing the fact. On my way up to Hawarden that night I recited as usual the Evening Prayer appointed for the day, and in the Second Lesson read the words: "Lord, suffer me first to go and bury my father and then I will follow Thee."

The days that followed were full of dignity and sorrow. It seemed incredible that my father was dead. He had just returned from Ireland, where he had paid a kind of semi-official visit to the Irish Protestant Church; he had seemed full of vitality. His last written words, found on his dressing-room table, were a draft of a letter to *The Times* on the subject of the Pope's Bull, just issued, condemning Anglican Orders as null and void. I celebrated the Communion service in Hawarden church before we left with the coffin for Canterbury, and gave Communion to Mr. Gladstone.

My father's body lay in its coffin before the altar, covered with the same pall which afterwards, I believe, lay on the coffin of Mr. Gladstone himself. The funeral was wonderfully impressive. A great storm of wind, rain, and thunder raged outside while we laid within the Cathedral, near the west doors, the body of the first Archbishop to be buried there since the Reformation. It still seemed incredible, as we went home, that we should not find that same vital and eager personality to greet us as we came back to Addington.

A week later my health suddenly and completely broke down and I was ordered to Egypt for the winter, at a week's notice. My last request to my Vicar, I remember, before hearing this news, had been to the effect that we might have a daily celebration in future in the church, in place of the two weekly ones that had been in use previously. But it was thought better not.

Canterbury Cathedral

Kemsing

CHAPTER TWO

UP to the time of my father's death I do not think
that a doubt had ever crossed my mind as to the
claims of Catholicism. Once, I remember, in Birdcage
Walk, as my father and I were riding back to Lambeth,
I said to him suddenly that I did not really understand
the phrase of the Creed, "I believe in the Holy Catholic Church." "For instance," I said, "are the Roman
Catholics a part of the Church of Christ?"

My father was silent for a moment. Then he said
that God only knew for certain who were or were not
within the Church: it might be perhaps that the Roman Catholics had so far erred in their doctrinal
beliefs as to have forfeited their place in the Body of
Christ. I suppose I was satisfied with his answer; for I do
not remember having considered the subject any further at the time. But within six weeks of my father's
death, matters began to appear to me in a new light,
and it was during the five months that I spent in the
East that for the first time the claims of the Catholic
Church showed themselves to me. It came about in
this way.

First, I believe, my contentment with the Church of England suffered a certain shock by my perceiving what a very small and unimportant affair the Anglican communion really was. There we were, travelling through France and Italy down to Venice, seeing in passing church after church whose worshippers knew nothing of us, or of our claims. I had often been abroad before, but never since I had formally identified myself with the official side of the Church of England. Now I looked at things through more professional eyes, and, behold! we were nowhere. Here was this vast continent apparently ignorant of our existence ! I believed myself a priest, yet I could not say so to strangers without qualifying clauses.

We arrived at Luxor at last, and found the usual hotel chaplain in possession; and I occasionally assisted him in the services. But it was all terribly isolated and provincial. Besides, he happened to be a strong Evangelical, and I had very little sense of having much in common with him. He would not have dreamed of describing himself as a "priest." (He was ultimately killed, by the way, with his whole family in the earthquake at Messina where he was acting as English chaplain.)

This growing discomfort was brought to a point one day when I was riding in the village by myself and went, purely by a caprice, into the little Catholic church there. It stood among the mud houses; there was no atmosphere of any European protection about it, and it had a singularly uninviting interior. There was in it a quantity of muslin and crimped paper and spangles. But I believe now that it was in there that for the first time anything resembling explicit Catholic faith stirred itself within me. The church was so obviously a part of the village life; it was on a level with the Arab houses; it was open; it was exactly like every other Catholic church, apart from its artistic shortcomings.

It was not in the least an appendage to European life, carried about (like an India rubber bath), for the sake of personal comfort and the sense of familiarity. Even if it did not possess one convert, it was at least looking in the right direction. I cannot say that I explicitly recognized all this at the time, but I am aware that here for the first time it occurred to me as seriously conceivable that Rome was right and we wrong; and my contempt for the Catholic Church began to take upon it a tinge of respectful fear. For my reassurance I made great friends with the Coptic priest and even, after my return to England, sent him a pair of brass candlesticks for his altar.

I began also to reason with myself a little and to fortify myself deliberately in my Anglican position. While in Cairo I had had two audiences of the schismatic Coptic Patriarch, and I now wrote to him, asking that I might be admitted to communion in the Coptic churches, desiring in some way to assure myself that we were not so much isolated as appeared. I did not care in the slightest whether the Copts were tainted by heresy or not (for there was a proverb about glass houses), but I did care that we Anglicans seemed so lonely and provincial. I began, in other words, for the first time to be aware of an instinct for Catholic communion. A national church seemed a poor affair abroad. The Patriarch did not answer, and I was left shivering.

As I came back alone through Jerusalem and the Holy Land, my discomfort increased. Here again, in the birthplace of Christendom, we were less than nothing. It is true that the Anglican Bishop was extremely kind, asked me to preach in his chapel, gave me a tiny gold cross (now hanging on an image of Our Lady), and obtained permission for me to celebrate the Communion in the Chapel of Abraham. Yet even this was not particularly reassuring. We were not allowed to use the Greek altar; a table was wheeled in, with the vestments provided by the Anglican "Confraternity of the Blessed Sacrament"; and there, distracted and unhappy, watched from the doorway by politely curious Greeks, I celebrated what I believed to be the divine mysteries, weighted down by a sense of loneliness.

In all the churches it was the same. Every Eastern heretical and schismatical sect imaginable took its turn at the altar of the Holy Sepulchre, for each had at least the respectability of some centuries behind it,— some sort of historical continuity. I saw strange, uncouth rites in Bethlehem. But the Anglican Church, which I had been accustomed to think of as the sound core of a rotten tree, this had no privileges anywhere; it was as if it did not exist; or, rather, it was recognised and treated by the rest of Christendom purely as a Protestant sect of recent origin. In a kind of self-assertion I began to wear my cassock publicly in the streets, to the consternation of some Irish Protestants whose acquaintance I had made, and with whom, by the way, I was distressed to think that I was in full communion. I even had a kind of disputation with a shopkeeper who said, in spite of my cassock, that he supposed I was not a priest, but a clergyman.

There were other clergymen in the party with whom I went up to Damascus, and two or three of us, every morning before starting, celebrated the Communion service in one of the tents. One of them, an American, a very devout and earnest man, not only said his office publicly on horseback, but had actually brought with him vestments, vessels, candlesticks, and wafers. These I used with a secret joy. I am happy to add that he, too, has been received into the Catholic Church and ordained to the priesthood.

At Damascus I received one more blow. I read in *The Guardian* that the preacher to whom I owed all my knowledge of distinctively Catholic doctrine, who had been the means of bringing me to my first confession, had made his submission to Rome. It is impossible to describe the horror and the shock that this was to me. I wrote to him from Damascus,—seeing even at the moment a kind of half-superstitious omen in the thought of what other conversion was associated with that place—a letter which, I am happy to think now, contained not a word of bitterness; but I received no answer. He has told me since that the unreproachful tone of the letter astonished him.

It was here, too, that once more my scheme for a Religious House revived; and, in a kind of defiance of the feelings that were beginning to trouble me, I arranged with a friend that its constitution and ceremonial were to be distinctively "English" by which I meant Caroline. We were to wear no eucharistic vestments, but full surplices and black scarfs, and were to do nothing in particular.

In this kind of mood I came back to England as to a haven of peace. There, I knew very well, I should not be troubled daily and hourly by evidences of my isolation, and I should find, moreover, exactly the atmosphere of peace and beauty for which I longed. I had been appointed assistant curate at Kemsing, the village where I had been initiated for the first time into the idea of orderly dogma; for it was necessary for me still to have but light work, owing to the state of my health.

It was an extraordinarily happy life there for about a year. The old church had been restored with exquisite taste, the music was really beautiful, the ceremonial dignified and "Catholic"; the vicarage where I lived with my friend was a charming house and always full of charming people; and in this entirely congenial atmosphere my troubles disappeared.

It was here that for the first time, after a second retreat preached by Father Maturin, my vicar regularly introduced linen vestments in which we celebrated the early Communion service every Sunday. We did not, however, use these or the lights and wafer bread at the midday celebrations, out of consideration to the very Low Church views of the squire, who, though himself a most charming and courteous old man, was something very like a fanatic on the side of ultra-Protestantism.

I often admired his extraordinary restraint as he entertained my vicar and myself in his beautiful old house— men whom he believed in his heart to be enemies of the Cross of Christ and unconscious co-operators with the Scarlet Woman of Rome. I did not much like this plan of presenting one form of worship on one occasion and another on another, for I grew daily in High Church principles and was congratulated by the clergyman in London to whom I went regularly to Confession about four times in the year, on my instincts for "Catholicism." I think it was at this period too that I joined three Ritualistic societies— the "English Church Union," the "Confraternity of the Blessed Sacrament," and the "Guild of All Souls." Meantime I was very happy at Kemsing.

It was quite possible, so long as one resolutely focused one's eyes to the proper objects, to believe that the Church of England was what she claimed to be, the spiritual mother of the English and a member of the Bride of Christ. I made several friends, whom, I am thankful to say, I retain to this day; I began to take pains with preaching: I did a good deal of work with children. The only reminders that ever came to me of external facts were occasional clerical meetings, at which one was reminded that all the world was not as Kemsing, and occasional and piercing little paragraphs in the newspapers to the effect that this man or that had been "received into the Roman Catholic Church."

It was not for about a year, however, that troubles reappeared, and I cannot remember what it was exactly which caused them. I used to have uncomfortable moments now and then, particularly after singing the choral celebration, when I wondered whether, after all, it was possible that I was wrong and that the ceremony in which I had taken part, rendered so beautiful by art and devotion, was no more than a subjective effort to assert our claim to what we did not possess. There was a brass in the chancel to the memory of one "Thomas de Hop", a pre-Reformation priest, and I used to ask myself sometimes what, honestly, Sir Thomas would think of it all. But all thoughts such as these I treated as temptations; I confessed them as sins; I read books on the Anglican side; I did my utmost in one or two cases to retain waverers; I thought to establish myself by contemptuous language against the "Italian Mission"—a phrase, I believe, originally coined by my father.

I remember especially one incident which shows how much these thoughts were in my mind at this time. I was present on the west front of St. Paul's Cathedral on the occasion of the Queen's Diamond Jubilee, but I think I was as much interested in the papal representative as in anyone else. I watched him eagerly and tried to make myself believe that he was impressed by the spectacle of the Church of England in her full glory. It was clearly an inspiriting sight, and I looked down with great enthusiasm at the Archbishops and Bishops, assembled on the steps, in positive copes. A rumour that they very nearly had consented to wear mitres as well caused great excitement in "Church Times" circles, and at least it was pleasant to see their shining head-gear of various descriptions. The Bishop of London, I remember, wore a superb gold skull-cap which was very nearly as good as a mitre, and I exulted to think of the tales the Papist would have to tell when he returned to his own arrogant friends. I was pleased also, a day or two later, on being told by a clergyman that he had actually been taken for a Roman priest in the crowd.

Strangely enough, however, I was not greatly affected by the papal decision on Anglican Orders that had appeared shortly before my leaving England. It had certainly been a blow, especially as I had been assured by one of the Anglican clergy who had gone to proffer information to the Commission sitting in Rome, that the decision would be in our favour; but I was never greatly moved by it. I was conscious of a certain bruised sensation in my soul whenever I thought of it, but never in all my Anglican days was I acutely affected either way by the condemnation.

It was during this time that I received my first confession—that of an Eton boy who was staying near and who became a Catholic a few months later. I remember my alarm at the thought of being disturbed during the ceremony, for, although confession was occasionally preached in the place, it was very seldom practised. So I locked the church door, trembling with excitement, heard the confession, and then went back to the house with a sense of awful and splendid guilt.

I began at last to be really restless. But even this restlessness, I perceived at the time, lay rather in the intuitive than the intellectual region. Though I read controversial books and comforted myself with Dr. Littledale's collection of sneers, I knew that this did not really touch the seat of my trouble: it lay deeper than that. It arose, I think, chiefly from two things: first, the sense of Anglican isolation that had been forced upon my notice abroad, and secondly from the strong case for Roman continuity with the pre-Reformation Church and the respective weakness of our own. I was reminded again of these things during a month in which I acted as Anglican chaplain at Cadenabbia. There was one other circumstance, besides those I have mentioned, which tended to in-crease my restlessness.

A few miles away from us was a convent of Angli-can nuns whose outward practice was simply in dis-tinguishable from that of a Catholic nunnery. On feasts unprovided for in *The Prayer Book*, such as Corpus Christi and the Assumption, it became the habit of certain clergy, both from London and in the country round, to attend the sacred festivities at this convent, and on half a dozen occasions I also took part.

The *Roman Missal* was used with all its ceremonies; and on the Feast of Corpus Christi a procession was formed according to the precise directions of Baldeschi in every detail. An altar of repose was set up in the beautiful garden and the *Pange lingua* sung. Now, these nuns were not playing at the Religious Life: they recited the night Office at night, according to the strictest observance —using of course the monastic Breviary—and lived a life of prayer in complete seclu-sion. But it was impossible to persuade myself, though of course I attempted to do so, that the atmosphere bore any resemblance at all to that of the Church of England in general.

The public was not admitted to these functions. I used to argue occasionally with the chaplain, who, as well as his successor, preceded me into the Catholic Church, criticizing certain details; but his answers, given with considerable learning—to the effect that, since the Church of England was Catholic, she had a right to all Catholic privileges— did not satisfy me; rather, the fact that Catholic privileges were obviously alien to her character seemed to imply that she was not Catholic; and I am sure that these visits, almost more than any thing else, began to emphasize to my mind the real gulf that separated me from Catholic Christendom. I pre-sented a silver lamp to the statue of Our Lady in this convent (it still hangs there), in a kind of endeavour to assert my Catholic aspirations.

So time went on and my restlessness with it. I began to diagnose my own case. I told myself that the life was too happy to be wholesome, and I set about future plans. I had learned by this time a certain effectiveness in preaching; I took part in a parochial mission, and at last was invited by the Canon Missioner of the diocese to join him definitely in mission work. But I had begun to have thoughts of the Religious Life, and was further dismayed to learn that, in the chapel of the house in Canterbury which we proposed to take, there must be no such ceremonial as that to which I had become accustomed. Honestly, I do not think that I was a mere "Ritualist," but it seemed to me evident that faith and its expression should go together, and that it would be an undue strain to preach a religion whose obvious and inseparable adjuncts were wanting. However, I decided to accept the invitation and went to see Archbishop Temple on the subject. He was quite kind and, after half an hour's conversation, quite peremptory. I was declared to be too young for such work, and I went back to Kemsing resolved to offer myself to the Community of the Resurrection, of whose fame I had heard again and again.

Within a few weeks I had an interview with Dr. Gore (now Bishop of Oxford) in his canon's house at Westminster, and was definitely accepted as a probationer. Dr. Gore was extremely kind and sympathetic; he seemed to understand my aspirations, and I was deeply impressed both by his own bearing and by the quiet religious atmosphere of the house. It seemed to me now that all my troubles were at an end.

I was intensely excited and pleased at the thought of the new life that was opening before me, and it became easier than ever to treat all Roman difficulties as diabolical temptations. I see now that my attention was distracted and my imagination filled with other visions; I was not really settled. But when I went up to Birkenhead for the annual retreat of the community with which my probation was to begin, I can sincerely say that no thought of henceforth ever leaving the Anglican communion appeared conceivable. I was to be launched in a new sea altogether; I was to live as the friars had lived five hundred years ago; I was to realize, though in an unexpected fashion, my old dreams of Llandaff and Damascus; I was to dedicate myself to God once and for all in the highest vocation open to man.

Thomas de Hop: 14th brass in
St Mary's Church, Kemsing

St Hugh and his swan

CHAPTER THREE

IT will be impossible for me ever to acknowledge adequately the debt of gratitude which I owe to the Community of the Resurrection, or the admiration which I always felt, and still feel, toward their method and spirit. All that it is possible to describe is the external aspect of their life and to hint only at the deep Christian charity and brotherliness and devotion that existed beneath it. It is true that they will not allow me to go and stay with them again as I should like to do, but individually, they are all most friendly, and, indeed such a visit might perhaps be really painful to them.

At the same time one must reflect that for an Anglican to become a Catholic is, even from the point of view of his old friends, a very different thing from the opposite process. For when a Catholic leaves the Church, those from whom he separates himself regard him as one who has left the Fold of Christ for the wilderness. It does not at all signify to what other body he may attach himself: he has left what his friends hold to be the One Body of Christ.

But when a High Churchman becomes a Catholic, on the Anglican theory all that he has done is to have transferred himself from one part of the Church to another; on the "Branch" theory, he has only shifted from one bough to the other; on the "Province" theory, to use yet more recent phraseology, he has only detached himself from Canterbury, not from the Church of Christ, as Anglicans understand it. It is true that he has, to their mind, become "schismatic"; worse, he has denied the validity of the Orders he once accepted; but it is impossible for his friends to regard him as an apostate in the simple sense of the word, and, to do them justice, they very seldom ever pretend do so. Certainly the Mirfield Brethren have never manifested to me in any way at all such an unjust discourtesy.

Next, before proceeding to give some account of the life we lived there, I must remark that I shall describe no more of the Life and Rule than could be observed by any visitor who stayed in the house. Every family has its "secrets," its little intimate ways and methods of life—I mean no more than that—and it would not be decent or loyal of me to treat of these. This inner domestic life, our relations with one another, our tone and atmosphere, were, I presume to think, singularly sweet and Christian. I suppose there must have been difficulties now and again, inseparable from the mutual intimacy of so many and various temperaments; but of those I have no remembrance at all. I remember only the extraordinary kindness and generosity that I always received.

We lived in a great house standing in its own gardens, at the top of a hill above the valley of the Calder. It was a somewhat smoky country; there were tall chimneys visible all round us, but the land that belonged to the house prevented any sensation of being pressed upon or crowded. Our external life was a modification of the old Religious Rules and resembled, so far as I understand, a kind of combination of the Redemptorist and the Benedictine. Some of the Brethren were engaged almost entirely in scholars' work—the editing of liturgical, hymnal, expository, and devotional works, and for the use of these there was a large library of about fifteen thousand volumes. The rest, who were the majority, spent about half the year in prayer and study at home, and the rest of it in evangelistic and mission work.

Our life ran on very simple and practical lines. We rose about a quarter past six and went at once to the chapel for Morning Prayer with the psalms of Prime, and the Communion service; at eight we breakfasted; at a quarter to nine we said Terce and made a meditation. Until ten minutes past one we worked in the library or our own rooms; then, after Sext and intercessions, we dined. In the afternoon we took exercise—walking or gardening; at half past four we said None and had tea. We worked again until seven, when we sang Evensong; we supped at the half hour, and, after a little recreation and work for an hour or two, we said Compline at a quarter to ten and went to our rooms. On Saturday mornings a chapter was held, at which, all kneeling, made a public confession of external breaches of the rule.

The community life was, when I first went there, in a somewhat transitional state: the Brethren were feeling their way in the direction of greater strictness; and by the time that I left them, four years later, a considerable development had taken place toward a more completely Religious character. Silence, for example, was extended gradually, until at last we did not speak from Compline in the evening until dinner the next day; manual work for so many hours a week was made an absolute rule; we broke up and carried coal, cleaned our own boots, and made our beds. My last manual task at Mirfield was the cutting and building of steps in the quarry that adjoined the house. Here I worked each afternoon and revolved meanwhile my interior difficulties.

The dress of the community, which was at first rather nondescript, developed more or less steadily in the direction of a habit, consisting of a double-breasted cassock girded with a leather belt. Originally, too, the head of the community was commonly addressed as "Senior," but when Dr. Gore was appointed Bishop of Birmingham and a new principal was elected, this title was supplanted by that of "Superior." The title "Father," which was at first somewhat discouraged, became later almost universal, although one or two members still disliked its significance. These changes, which the majority, including myself, ardently desired, were not carried out without protest on the part of three or four members; and, although nothing resembling bitterness ever made its appearance, one Brother at any rate found himself compelled to withdraw at last at the time of the annual renewal of vows.

It is more difficult to explain these vows. Mr. George Russell delivered more than one genial blow at them in *The Cornhill Magazine* and elsewhere. We were supposed to pledge ourselves to celibacy only until such time as we wanted to marry. Roughly speaking, the probation lasted normally for one full year—from July to July— after which, if the probationer received the votes of the community, he made his profession. This consisted of an absolute promise to observe the rule of the community for thirteen months, and an expression of his deliberate intention to remain in it for life. Profession, therefore, was not in the least of the nature of a mere experiment: it meant practically a life intention, though an escape was provided if the life for any reason became intolerable. The Rule itself was built upon the vows of poverty, chastity, and obedience, all three of which were integrally woven into it. The life was less rigid, therefore, than that of the ordinary Catholic Orders, but more rigid than that of such Congregations as the Oratorian.

We numbered at that time about fourteen members, all of whom were in the full Orders of the Church of England, and all of whom had had experience of parish work. We had no lay-brothers, but the necessary household duties which we did not do ourselves were done by three or four servants. Now, however, the numbers of the community have risen to between twenty and thirty; a large College of the Resurrection has been built in the grounds for the education of poor men for the ministry; a hostel has been opened in Leeds and a community house in Johannesburg; lay-brothers also, I understand, have been tried as an experiment. A chapel also, I believe, is in course of erection; but while I was there we used a large room in the house, very skilfully and beautifully adapted for worship.

Our worship was really dignified and devotional, but did not in its ritual rise above the ordinary level of the Anglo-Catholic party in general. We used vestments, at first of linen, but later, first by means of a gift made through me to the community, we began to substitute coloured vestments. We used incense unceremonially, in accordance with the Lambeth "opinions," and for our music sang, for the most part, unaccompanied plain-song adapted to *The Book of Common Prayer*. Frankly, we did not sing well, but we did our best; and I shall not easily forget the sense of beauty and mystery at our sung celebrations early on Sunday mornings. The altar was on the approved English type with "riddels"; two candles stood upon the altar, two more upon the posts of the curtains, and two more in standards. We had a sanctuary lamp, which I always disliked, since it did not signify any thing in particular.

It is impossible to describe the happiness which I enjoyed at Mirfield. For about one year I did very little external preaching and busied myself almost entirely in theological study and prayer. My "novice master" was a sympathetic and competent guide of souls and, although I did not go to Confession to him, I always felt that he was able and willing to help me. For a while there was only one other probationer besides myself— an Irishman of great eloquence and fervour, who developed into an extremely capable mission-preacher, but who, later, left the community and married. We were thrown together a great deal, and I found in him an open enthusiasm of faith and confidence in the Church of England (alternating with depressions, however) which did much to reassure my own.

When the time of my profession drew near, however, I began somewhat to distrust my suitability for the life. It was not that I was troubled with Roman difficulties, for these had practically vanished; but, owing to a certain resolution passed by the community in view of a crisis in the Church of England, I began to think that my position was too "advanced" for my contentment in the house. By this time I had learned to hold practically all the dogmas of the Catholic Church except that of the Pope's Infallibility. I studied and analyzed Lehm-kuhl's *Moral Theology*, omitting as irrelevant all sections dealing with the Supreme Pontiff. I said my Rosary regularly; I invoked the saints; I thought that the word "Transubstantiation" best expressed the reality of Our Lord's presence in the Sacrament; I held that Penance was the normal means by which post-baptismal mortal sin was remitted; I used the word " Mass " freely at home.

These doctrines, too, I preached in veiled language, and found that by them, and them alone, could I arouse the enthusiasm of congregations—these doctrines, at least, set forth round the adorable Person of

Christ, which, remembering the lessons of *John Inglesant*, I endeavoured to make the centre of my teaching. I remember, for example, being told once by an indignant curate that my doctrine seemed "a mixture of Romanism and Wesleyanism"—an accusation that brought me the greatest satisfaction. The community in general, on the other hand, seemed to me at that time to be over-cautious, to desire to dissociate themselves from the extreme party in the Church of England; and it was to this party that I now belonged.

The end was that I postponed my profession for one year, in order to test myself yet further. But that year removed my difficulties. I began to be more and more encouraged in mission-work and to find that my quiet life at Mirfield gave me a power that I could obtain in no other way. It is hard for Catholics to believe it, but it is a fact that as an Anglican I had far longer hours in the confessional than I have ever had in the Catholic Church, though, of course, this is to be accounted for by the fact that since becoming a Catholic I have never preached a regular mission. In one London parish, for instance, for about four days at the end of a mission, my brother-missioner and I interviewed people, hearing confessions and recommending resolutions and rules of life, for over eleven hours each day; two more hours were occupied in delivering sermons to vast congregations.

This, however, was after my profession. Yet everywhere it seemed as if an immense work was waiting to be done. We came from our quiet life red-hot with zeal and found everywhere men and women who seemed to have been waiting for us in an extraordinary manner. We saw conversions everywhere; we saw sinners changed by the power of God, children enkindled and taught, the luke-warm set on fire, and the obstinate broken down. It was impossible to doubt that the grace of God was at work here; and if the Church of England was capable of being used as a vessel of so much honour, why any longer need one doubt of her divine mission? And since that was so, and since also I had found such extreme happiness and inspiration in the life at Mirfield, why should I any longer hesitate to commit myself to it?

Before my profession I was asked by Dr. Gore, greatly to my surprise, whether I was in any danger of lapsing to Rome. I honestly told him "No, so far as I could see," and in July, 1901, I took the step without alarm. It was an extraordinarily happy day. I obtained a new cassock for the purpose, which, strangely enough, I am wearing at this moment, adapted to the Roman cut. My mother came up and was present in the tiny ante-chapel. I was formally installed; my hand was kissed by the brethren; I pronounced my vows and received Communion as a seal and pledge of stability. In the afternoon I drove out with my mother in a kind of ecstasy of contentment.

Then once more I set to work. I think the most trying part of my external work lay in the strange varieties of doctrine and ceremonial with which I became acquainted. As a rule, of course, we were asked to conduct missions only in parishes where our standard of belief and preaching was accepted. (We were not, I believe, however, regarded as quite satisfactory by the extreme party of Ritualists, and this, no doubt, was partly owing to Dr. Gore's position. He was identified, rightly or wrongly, with the High Liberal School; he was supposed to be unsound on the doctrine of the Incarnation; his views on Higher Criticism were considered dangerous; he was thought a little extravagant on the subject of Christian Socialism. And all this, of course, was a certain distress to me, since on those three points I was not at all one of his disciples.)

But what was far more trying was my experience of less advanced churches where I gave an occasional sermon, and where the clergyman did not feel that the merely passing presence of a "Brother" would compromise him irreparably. Here, as well as in the three churches of Mirfield, which we attended as we liked on Sunday evenings, I found all kinds of teaching and ceremonial. In one church they would wear elaborate stoles but no vestments, with doctrine to correspond; in another, vestments would be used at services to which the important Protestants did not come; teaching on the Real Presence would be skilfully veiled, and Penance would be referred to in a hasty aside as the "Sacrament of reconciliation," or taught explicitly only to a favoured few at some small guild service. And, of course, it must be remembered that even so we did not experience a tenth of the further divisions and schools of thought in the Church of England—divisions of which, however, it was impossible to be ignorant.

It was easy after a little experience to diagnose, almost at a glance at the clergyman or his church, the exact doctrinal level of the teaching given; and in less advanced places it was my custom to preach the love of Jesus Christ or the joy of penitence or the Fatherhood of God with all the fervour I had, in the hope that these truths would find their normal outcome some day in those who heard me.

On the only occasion on which I preached in Westminster Abbey I put all my energies into attempting to set forth the Person of Jesus Christ as the centre of all religion, leaving all other doctrines to take care of themselves. I was not as courageous as another member of the community, who, in the same circumstances, denounced the "dead altars" of that place of worship! But this was all very unsatisfactory, and gradually, no doubt, though I did not realise it at the

time, began to shake my confidence once more in the
Church of England as a Divine Teacher. I used to hurry
back to Mirfield as to a refuge; for there at least there
was peace and tolerable unanimity. My intellectual
escape from the difficulty seemed to me, however,
quite convincing. It was as follows.

Originally, as a "Moderate High Church man," I
had held that the Church of England, in her appeal
and in her supposed resemblance to the "Primitive"
Church, was the most orthodox body in Christendom;
that Rome and the East on the one side had erred
through excess; and the Nonconformist bodies on the
other through defect and these, further, through their
loss of episcopal succession, had forfeited any corpo-
rate place in the Visible Body of Christ. But this
doctrinal position had long ago broken down under
me. First, I had seen the impossibility of believing that
for about a thousand years the promises of Christ had
failed—between, that is, the fifth or sixth century and
the Reformation period—and that corruption during
all this space of time had marred the original purity of
the Gospel.

Next, I had begun to perceive that in the Church of
Christ there must be some Living Voice which, if not
actually infallible, must at least be taken to be such—
some authoritative person or Council who could pass
judgment upon new theories and answer new questions. I had attempted, strangely enough, to find this
Living Voice in *The Book of Common Prayer* and the
Articles—to seek in them, that is to say, a final imme-
diate interpreter of remote Primitive and Apostolic
Faith.

But now I had learned the fallacy of such an attempt, since even these formularies could be, and
were, taken in completely divergent senses: the Ritualist, for instance, finds that the Prayer Book Catechism teaches the Objective and Real Presence of

Christ in the Sacrament, and the Low Churchman claims it as teaching Receptionism. Then, when I had looked despairingly to the only elements in the Church of England which bear any resemblance at all to a Living Voice—the decisions of Convocation, the resolutions of Pan-Anglican Conferences, and the utterances of Bishops—I found, either that these were divided amongst themselves, or that they refused to answer, or, at the worst, that they answered in a manner which I could not reconcile with what I was convinced was the Christian Faith.

The "Moderate High Church" theory, then, had broken down so far as I was concerned, and I had been forced, it seemed to me, both by logic and the pressure of circumstances, to seek some other theory as the foundation of my faith. This I found, for the time, in the Ritualistic School. It was as follows.

The Catholic Church, I now premised, consisted of those bodies of Christians retaining the Catholic Creeds and the Apostolic ministry. Roughly speaking, these comprised Rome, Moscow, and Canterbury, together with a few detached bodies, such as the "Old Catholics," of whom I knew very little. This "Catholic Church," therefore, did have a speaking voice of a kind: she spoke through her silent consensus. Where Rome, Moscow, and Canterbury agreed, there was the explicit voice of the Holy Spirit; where they dogmatically disagreed, there was the field for private opinion. Now Canterbury occasionally faltered in her witness, but it was at least arguable, I thought, that she had never spoken positive heresy. (I explained away the statements of the Thirty-Nine Articles in the manner familiar to Anglican controversialists.)

Therefore, where Canterbury was silent, her sense must be taken to be that of the rest of "Catholic Christendom." This was a very convenient theory, for by it I was able to embrace practically all the doctrines of the Catholic Church proper, except that of Papal Infallibility and the concurrent necessity of external communion with Rome; and I was able to feel that I had behind me the silent toleration, though not necessarily the explicit authority, of my own communion; and, what was far weightier, the authority of Christ's Church as a whole.

It will be seen, then, that I had travelled far from the old Tractarian position of the appeal to the Ancient Undivided Church. On the contrary, divisions made no difference to me; schism was practically impossible so long as the Apostolic ministry and Creeds were maintained; and I had travelled even farther from my old East London position of believing that the Church of England was the sound core of a rotten tree. When, therefore, again in the course of these papers I shall have occasion to refer to this theory of mine—which, as a matter of fact, held me altogether now until it broke beneath me suddenly— I shall call it by the name of the "Diffusive Theory."

In its shadow I invoked saints, having little pictures of them, drawn by myself, with a statue of Our Lady; adored Christ in His Sacrament, and, indeed, began to learn for the first time a real spirit of Catholic submission. If once a doctrine could be proposed to me with the authority of the Church Diffusive behind it, I should set aside all my predispositions and accept it whole-heartedly.

For a while I was puzzled somewhat to interpret to myself the manner by which this authority actually did speak to the unlearned who were incapable of research into what was or was not covered by the theory; but gradually I evolved an idea. As the unlearned Roman Catholic layman applies to a clergyman who acknowledges the authority of the Roman Pontiff and is in communion with him, so the unlearned layman of the Church Diffusive should apply to a clergyman who acknowledged the authority of the Church Diffusive; and it is perfectly true that if such laymen actually did so, they would, as a matter of fact, find a very tolerable unanimity. In one of my last struggles in 1903 I did propose this view, as a possible escape, to my Superior; but I was told that it was impossible. Neither then nor now do I understand why; for, granted the first theory, the application of it seems the only logical or practical conclusion.

There, then, I settled down for nearly two years as a professed member of the community, during about one year extremely happy and confident—except once or twice when my old difficulties suddenly recurred for a while and then left me again—finding, as I have said before, a brotherliness and companionship that is beyond appreciation.

Still, in my dreams sometimes I am back at Mirfield, though never, thank God, as an Anglican! Once, I remember, Cardinal Merry del Val had been appointed Superior and had received the submission of the community, and I, too, was back there, happy and exultant, standing in the library and laughing with pure joy. Once I was there, I thought, as a Catholic priest, and found that, although there should have been a barrier of shyness between the community and myself, there was none. We stood together in the hall and talked as four years ago.

Yet I never have been back there, although I should like to go for a visit, even without the Cardinal; but the community judges otherwise. It was here, too, that I first began to systematize my devotion and to attempt the art of meditation, and it was here that God rewarded me abundantly for my poor efforts. He was preparing me, as I see now very well, for the great decision that He was to set before me so soon.

CHAPTER FOUR

I THINK that it was in the summer and autumn of 1902 that I began to write a book called *The Light Invisible*. Some stories of my eldest brother's had put the idea into my mind, and I began to write these little by little, as I had time. The stories, which are of a semi-mystical and imaginative nature, centre round a man whom I call a "Catholic priest," and I have been asked again and again whether I intended this man to be a Catholic or an Anglican. My only answer is that I intended him to be neither in particular.

My theory of the Church Diffusive more and more drove me to obliterate, in my thoughts as well as in my preaching, any distinction between what I believed to be merely various parts of Christ's mystical Body, and in *The Light Invisible*, accordingly, I aimed deliberately at the water-line. For by this time, too, my difficulties were once more recurring, so I tried not to indicate by the slightest hint the communion to which my hero belonged. This I see now to have been more significant than I realized at the time: I did not have that supreme confidence in the Church of England which would naturally have made me content to call him an Anglican and have done with it.

Before, during, and after the writing of this book I was more and more becoming interested in mystical lines of thought. I put away from me the contemplation of cold-cut dogma and endeavoured to clothe it with the warm realities of spiritual experience; and in the book itself I attempted to embody dogma rather than to express it explicitly.

I have been asked whether any of the stories were "true," and to that I have no answer except that the book itself does not claim to be anything other than fiction. I think that to some extent I must have been successful in hitting the water-line between Catholicism and Anglicanism, since the book still sells well both among Catholics and Anglicans. Yet I was undoubtedly still deeply affected by Anglicanism; for when I wrote a story in the book about a nun's praying before the Blessed Sacrament, I had in my mind an Anglican convent which I knew, and was staying at the time in the clergy house of St. Cuthbert's, Kensington, where the Sacrament is reserved. Yet at the same time I remember dissociating myself internally from any actual self committing as to what I intended; it was not that I at all disbelieved in Anglican Orders at that time, yet I never felt that the repudiation of them would be a serious obstacle to my submission to the Church.

The popularity of the book—or rather, the classes of persons who, respectively, like and dislike the book—appears to me rather significant. It still sells very considerably amongst Anglicans; and, to a very much lesser degree, among Catholics. It is, of course, also perfectly natural that a certain type of Anglican should enjoy shaking his head over my sad deterioration, both literary and spiritual, since I left the Church of England; but, even apart from this controversial device, it is quite true that Anglicans, as a class, prefer it infinitely to anything else that I have ever written; while most Catholics, and myself amongst them, think that *Richard Raynal, Solitary* is very much better written and very much more religious.

In fact, for myself, I dislike, quite intensely, *The Light Invisible*, from the spiritual point of view. I wrote it in moods of great feverishness and in what I now recognize as a very subtle state of sentimentality; I was striving to reassure myself of the truths of religion, and assumed, therefore, a positive and assertive tone that was largely insincere; the very careful, trimmed style of the book is an evidence of this. Further, it is, I think, rather a mischievous book in very distinct ways, since it implies that what I then strove to believe was spiritual intuition—and what is really nothing but imagination—must be an integral element in religious experience; and that "sight" —or rather personal realization—must be the mode of spiritual belief rather than the simple faith of a soul that receives divine truth from a divine authority.

The Catholic atmosphere is, on the other hand, something quite apart from all this. For Catholics it is almost a matter of indifference as to whether or no the soul realizes, in such a manner as to be able to visualize, the facts of revelation and the principles of the spiritual world: the point is that the Will should adhere and the Reason assent. But for Anglicans, whose theology is fundamentally unreasonable, and amongst whom Authority is, really, non-existent, it becomes natural to place the centre of gravity rather in the Emotions, and to "mistake," therefore, as Mrs. Craigie says somewhere, "the imagination for the soul." The Reason, for them, must be continually suppressed even in its own legitimate sphere; the Will must be largely self-centred. There remains then, for them, the experience of feeling, only, as the realm in which spirituality operates. My own rather exaggerated dislike of the book, arises, I suppose, from a reaction against these unrealities amongst which I lived for so long.

Here, although it is something of an anachronism, I should like to explain how I managed to hold the apparently unsatisfactory position of believing in Anglican Orders and yet contemplating with equanimity the time when I might have to repudiate them. Later on, when matters were serious, my Superior told me that he could not understand it; that I appeared to be indifferent to spiritual experience; that it was a terrible thing for me to contemplate repudiating all the graces which I had received and bestowed through the Sacraments of the Church of England. Yet, honestly, I did not find it a burden.

The way I expressed it to myself was this. There are two things in the reception of grace—the fact and the mode. The fact is a matter of spiritual intuition; the mode, of intellectual apprehension. As regarded the former—the actual communications between Our Lord and my soul—granted above all at moments of great solemnity, I neither had nor have the slightest doubt. Without any sort of hesitation I still say that the times of Communion in the chapel at Mirfield and elsewhere, and of Anglican Confession, will always be among the most sacred of my life; to deny reality to them would be indeed to betray Our Lord and repudiate His love. But the mode is quite another matter. While I was in the Church of England I accepted, practically to the very end, her authoritative statement that I was a priest, and the consequent deduction that the grace of her ordinances was actually sacramental. But when I submitted to Rome, I accepted with far greater security, with an internal as well as an external consent, her authoritative statement that I never was a priest at all. She has never asked me to repudiate anything else on the subject or to assert anything so entirely blasphemous and absurd as that which

Anglicans occasionally pretend of her—namely, the diabolical or even illusive nature of the grace that God bestows on those who are in good faith. In my Confessions in the Church of England I, at any rate, made acts of contrition and did my best to comply with the Sacrament of Penance; in my Communions I lifted up my heart toward the Bread of Life; and, therefore, Our Lord could not be the Rewarder of those that seek Him if He had not visited me in response.

All this, I think, I saw quite plainly long before my submission was imminent; and the fact that I was told, upon explaining, that I was splitting hairs, did not trouble me. I understood that a hair's breadth is sometimes a great distance. About Jurisdiction I neither knew nor cared anything.

In the summer of 1902 I told my mother, in a walk, that I had had Roman difficulties, but that they were gone again; and at the same time I promised her that, should they recur, I would tell her at once. Sometime between that and Christmas I had to redeem my promise. I can never feel enough gratitude that I did so, and that she received my confidence in the way that she did. I kept both her and my Superior informed of every step of the process through which I went, and carried out their recommendations to the letter; I read all the books I was given on the Anglican side, and consulted all the living authorities proposed to me. Both my mother and my Superior treated me throughout with the utmost kindness and consideration. Even from secondary motives I am thankful that I acted as I did; for both of them, when my submission had taken place and, as usually happens in such cases, a flood of accusations as regarded underhandedness and deceit poured in, informed their correspondents that such accusations were entirely untrue.

I think it must have been in the October of this year that I reached such a pitch of distress that, with my Superior's permission, I wrote to a distinguished priest an account of all my difficulties. (I will presently try to indicate what they were.) His answer was very surprising to me then. It is less surprising to me now, since the priest in question has, finally, died out of Catholic communion. He defined for me very carefully the doctrine of Papal Infallibility and the exact sense put upon it by the general feeling of the Church and advised me to wait. He told me—what I have since found to be not the case—that while the "minimizers" seemed to have been victorious as regards the wording of the Vatican decree upon Papal Infallibility, it was the "maximizers" who had been winning ever since; and he added that although he himself, as a "minimizer," felt himself individually justified in remaining where he was, he would not feel himself justified in officially receiving anyone into the Church except on the terms that now prevailed, viz., on "maximizing" principles: he added that "maximizing" views were impossible to persons of reason.

The conclusion, therefore, practically, was that I had better remain where I was. One sentence in his letter gave me, I think, an inkling into the objective disloyalty of his position: I had asked him to remember me in his Mass and, in return, he begged to be remembered in mine. After my reception into the Church he wrote to me again, asking how I had surmounted the difficulty which he had indicated. I answered by saying that I could not be deterred by such elaborate distinctions from uniting myself to what I was convinced was the divinely appointed centre of Unity and that I had simply accepted the Decree in the sense in which the Church herself had uttered and accepted it.

For a little while, however, his first letter quieted and reassured me, and I was only too willing to be reassured. My Superior, too, remarked that I could not very well have a plainer indication of God's Will that I should remain in the communion where He had placed me. The very fact that I had written to a priest and received an answer of discouragement seemed to me then—and to him still, I imagine—an evident sign of where my duty lay. It seemed to show too that even within the Roman Church wide divergences of opinion prevailed, and that there was not there that Unity for which I had looked. The ultimate history of the priest in question, his excommunication, and his death outside the Church showed, of course, that such is not the case, and that men are not allowed to represent the Church who misrepresent, even in good faith, her teaching.

I was reassured, then, for only a very little while. Almost immediately my doubts recurred. I had preaching engagements that would naturally occupy me most of the winter, and these were now imminent. I asked leave to withdraw from them, but my Superior thought it better not; and, looking back upon it, it seems to me now that the best chance of silencing the clamour of my ideas did indeed lie in active work.

I preached a mission or two and returned to Mirfield; I went home for Christmas and once more came back to the Community. By this time I was really in sore distress. I had even asked a recent convert, lately ordained priest, and a great friend of mine, who came to stay at my mother's house in November, to pray for me, and I had put one or two difficulties to him to see what he would answer. But my distress quieted again ever so little in the atmosphere of Mirfield, and once more I was sent out, very unwillingly, to preach a mission or two and conduct Holy Week services and discourses in a church in the south of England.

On Good Friday I preached the "Three Hours," and on Easter Day evening for the last time I stood in an Anglican pulpit and preached on the appearance of Our Lord to the penitent Magdalene. As I came down the steps at the end, I think I knew what would happen. I then returned to Mirfield, exhausted physically, mentally, and spiritually.

It does not seem to me that Catholic controversialists as a body in the least realize what Anglicans have to go through before they can make their submission. I am not speaking of external sufferings—of the loss of friends, income, position, and even the barest comforts of life. From such losses as these I was spared, though it is true that the leaving of the Community was about the most severe external trial I have ever undergone—I kissed, in Greek fashion, the doorposts of my room as I left it for the last time; yet I did not, I think, lose the personal friendship of the individual members; I still see them occasionally and hear from them.

I mean rather the purely internal conflict. One is drawn every way at once; the soul aches as in intolerable pain; the only relief is found in a kind of passionless Quietism. To submit to the Church seems, in prospect, to be going out from the familiar and the beloved and the understood into a huge, heartless wilderness, where one will be eyed and doubted and snubbed. Certainly that is largely an illusion; yet it is, I think, the last emotional snare spread by Satan; and I think that he is occasionally aided in spreading it by the carelessness of Catholic controversialists.

Two incidents of the kind very nearly put out the dawning light of faith in me altogether. I will not describe them, but in both cases it was a careless sentence snapped out by a good, sincere priest in a public discourse. When a soul reaches a certain pitch of conflict, it ceases to be absolutely logical; it is rather a very tender, raw thing, with all its fibres stretched to agony, shrinking from the lightest touch, desiring to be dealt with only by Hands that have been pierced. Then it is handled roughly, pushed this way and that by a man who understands nothing, who lives in a bright light toward which the sensitive soul of the convert is reaching out with unutterable pain. Is it any wonder that again and again the miserable thing creeps back into the twilight sooner than bear any more, believing that a half-light with charity must be nearer to God's Heart than the glare of a desert? . . .

Now, intellectually considered, the outline of my difficulties was as follows—I have written out the arguments that especially prevailed with me in a little pamphlet which I published soon after my submission—and it was on these subjects in particular that, ever since the October of the previous year, I had read steadily and swiftly when ever I had an opportunity. Now once more I gave myself up entirely to reading and prayer.

First, there was the general, and what I may call the ideal, conception of God's plan. Secondly, there were the actual realistic facts about me in the world. Let me take the second first, since the second was prior in time, though not in importance to my mind. The facts were as follows.

I accepted Christianity as the Revelation of God. This was my axiom which I am not concerned now to defend. I accepted, too, *The Bible* as an inspired and a divinely safeguarded record of the facts of this Revelation. But I had come to see, as I have already explained, the need of a Teaching Church to preserve and to interpret the truths of Christianity to each succeeding generation. It is only a dead religion to which written records are sufficient; a living religion must be able to adapt itself to changing environment without losing its own identity.

One thing, therefore, is absolutely certain— that if Christianity is, as I believe it, a real Revelation, the Teaching Church must at any rate know her own mind with regard to the treasure committed to her care, and supremely on those points on which the salvation of her children depends. She may be undecided and permit divergent views on purely speculative points; she may allow her theologians, for instance, to argue, unchecked, for centuries as to the modes by which God acts, or as to the best philosophical terms for the elucidation of mysteries, or as to the precise limits of certain of her own powers and the manners of their exercise.

But in things that directly and practically affect souls— with regard to the fact of grace, its channels, the things necessary for salvation, and the rest—she must not only know her mind, but must be constantly declaring it, and no less constantly silencing those who would obscure or misinterpret it.

Now this was not at all the case with the Communion in which I found myself. I was an official of a church that did not seem to know her own mind even on matters directly connected with the salvation of the soul. It was my duty to preach and practise the system of redemption which God had given through the life and death of Jesus Christ, and that system I knew very well to be a sacramental one.

Yet when I looked about me for a clear statement as to that system I did not find it. It was true that many individuals taught and accepted what I did; there were societies to which I belonged—the "English Church Union" and the "Confraternity of the Blessed Sacrament" —that were practically unfaltering in these respects; but it was impossible to say that the authorities of my Church were equally clear.

To take one single vital point—the doctrine of Penance. I was really ignorant as to whether or not it was permissible to teach that this was, normally, essential to the forgiveness of mortal sin. Practically all the Bishops denied this, and a few of them denied the power of absolution altogether. But, even granting that my views were tolerated—which really they were not in any authoritative way—the fact that mutually exclusive views were also tolerated was an evidence that mine were not enjoined. I was teaching, at the best, my private opinion upon a point that was still officially indefinite. I was teaching as a certainty what was officially uncertain. It was becoming, then, the clearer I saw this, more and more impossible to say that the Church of England required sacramental confession.

The way in which many clergy escape from this dilemma is very simple. They appeal not to the living voice of the Church of England, but to her written formularies, and they explain those formularies in accordance with their own views. But I was finding it hard to do this sincerely, because I had begun to see that a written formulary can never be decisive in a church where that formulary can be taken in more than one sense—as it undoubtedly is—and the authorities not only will not decide as to which is the true sense, but actually tolerate senses that are mutually exclusive.

More and more I was beginning to see the absolute need of a living authority who can continue to speak as new interpretations of her former words contend for the mastery. A church that appeals merely to ancient written words can be no more at the best than an antiquarian society.

Of course I was told to be content with my own interpretation; but that was impossible. My point was that, since my interpretation was disputed, I could not teach it as authoritative. Dr. Pusey was held up to me, also Mr. Keble, and others. But I said that I could not rest on the authority of individuals however eminent, for there were other individuals equally eminent who held opposing views. By one or two advisers I was told that those points were unessential; that the main facts of the Christian Creed were all that were absolutely necessary, and that upon these the Anglican witness was clear enough.

My answer was that those points were the most practical of all, that they concerned not remote theological propositions, but the actual details of Christian life. Might I or might I not tell penitents that they were bound to confess their mortal sins before Communion? This is only one instance out of many, for on all sides were the same questions. I saw round me a Church which, even if tolerable in theory, was intolerable in practice. Her children lived and died by tens of thousands actually ignorant of what I believed to be the Catholic Gospel —ignorant not merely through neglect, but through the deliberate instruction of men who were as fully accredited ministers as myself— children of hers, too, who desired nothing more than to learn and obey her precepts and who might have had every opportunity of doing so.

Then on the other side there was the Church of Rome. Now, I think I had heard at various times all the theoretical or historical arguments that could possibly be brought against her claims; but, regarded practically, there was no question. Her system worked. It might be that it worked mechanically and superstitiously, but it was there. I remember in a private conversation comparing the rival systems to two differently laid fires.

The Anglican system was as a man applying a match to a tumbled heap of fuel: where there was personal zeal and sincerity, a flame certainly shot up, souls were warmed and lighted; but when the personal influence or the private "Catholic" views of the individual clergymen were removed, all was left as before.

In the Roman system, however, it was very different; there might be slackness and lack of piety, but, at any rate, the fire burned quite apart from the individual influence, because the fuel was laid in order. Whether or no a priest was careless or slothful or even lax in his private views made no essential difference;

his flock knew what was necessary for salvation and how to obtain it. The smallest Roman Catholic child knew precisely how to be reconciled to God and to receive His grace.

Secondly, there was the question of Catholicity itself. The Anglican theory was simply bewildering, as I looked at it from a less provincial standpoint. I had no notion as to who was the rightful Bishop, say, of Zanzibar; it would depend, I thought, chiefly on the question as to which Communion, the Roman or the Anglican, happened to have landed first on the African coast! In fact, Jurisdiction was represented to me as a kind of pious race-game. In Ireland I knew very well that I was in communion with persons who, according to my personal views, were simply heretics, and out of communion with persons who believed, so far as practical religion went, exactly what I myself believed.

On the other hand, the Roman theory was simplicity itself. "I am in communion," the Romanist could say with St. Jerome, "with Thy Blessedness— that is, with the Chair of Peter. On this rock I know that the Church is built." The Roman theory worked, the Anglican did not.

Yet, of course, these considerations did not settle the question. Our Lord, I was told, spoke often in mysteries; He refused to cut knots by direct and simple answers. It might very well be that the golden thread of His divine plan ran in these days through tangled woods and undergrowth, and that the plain highway was but the monument of man's impatience and lack of faith.

On these points, then, though they predisposed me toward the Catholic Church, it was necessary to read a great deal. There were, besides, other points flowing from them that needed elucidation. How, for example, was it possible that dogmas binding now should not have been binding a hundred years ago? How about the Immaculate Conception —which, as a matter of private opinion, I was perfectly ready to accept—and Papal Infallibility? And then, finally, after innumerable gropings, there always remained the old vexed business of the Petrine Texts and the patristic comments upon them.

This, then, I began to see more and more overwhelmingly: that it is possible, from the huge complications of history, philosophy, exegesis, natural law, and the rest—and, in fact, every single method of God's indications of His Will— to make out a case for almost any theory under the sun. The materials from which I was obliged, all incompetent, to judge, were as a vast kaleidoscope of colours. I might say that the main scheme was red and that the rest were accidental, or that it was blue or green or white. Each man, I perceived, had a natural inclination to one theory and tended to select it.

It was certainly possible to make out a claim for Anglicanism or the Papacy or Judaism or the system of the Quakers. And on this, almost despairing, I had to set to work. One thing, however, began to emerge ever so slowly; namely, that intellect alone could prove very little. The puzzle which God had flung to me consisted of elements which needed for their solution not the head only, but the heart, the imagination, the intuitions; in fact, the entire human character had to deal with it. It was impossible to escape wholly from natural prejudice, but I must do my best.

I must step back a little from the canvas and regard the affair as a whole, not bend over it with a measuring-rod and seek to test the elusive ethereal whole by but one faculty of my nature. Yet at the beginning I only half-realized this and plunged, therefore, blindly into the bewildering maze of controversy.

I should be sorry to have to make a complete list of

all the controversial works which I read during the last eight months of my Anglican days. I devoured everything I could find, on both sides. I read Dr. Gore's books, Salmon *On Infallibility*, Richardson, Pusey, Ryder, Littledale, Puller, Darwell Stone, Percival, Mortimer, Mallock, Rivington. I studied with care a brilliant MS. book on Elizabethan history; I made profuse notes; and, supremely, I read Newman's *Development of Christian Doctrine* and Mozley's answer. I also looked up various points in the Fathers, but with a kind of despair, since I knew I was wholly incompetent to decide where great scholars disagreed.

I must confess that I became bewildered and hopeless. Was it not better for me to relinquish this dusty search and remain peacefully where God's Providence had placed me? After all, there had been an extraordinary revival of Catholic life in the Church of England and I had, from the nature of my mission work, been peculiarly privileged to see its effects. Would it not be a kind of sin against the Holy Ghost to turn my back on the visibly solid work of grace, in search for what might be no more than a brilliant phantom?

Pilgrims' Way

CHAPTER FIVE

GRADUALLY, however, three things drew out of the clamouring mob of ideas and authors. The first was a thought. It had been put to me by my Superior that I was surely incurring the guilt of pride in venturing to set up my opinion against the views of men, such as Dr. Pusey or Mr. Keble— men infinitely my superiors in goodness, learning, and experience. They had been into all these questions far more profoundly than I could ever hope to go, and had come to the conclusion that the claims of Rome were unjustified, and that the Church of England was, at any rate, a part of Christ's Church.

And then I suddenly realized clearly what I had only suspected before; namely, that if the Church of Christ was, as I believed it to be, God's way of salvation, it was impossible that the finding of it should be a matter of shrewdness or scholarship; otherwise salvation would be easier for the clever and leisured than for the dull and busy. As for the holiness of men like Dr. Pusey— after all, "Christ came into this world to save sinners." Two or three texts of Scripture began to burn before me. "A highway shall be there," wrote Isaias; "... the redeemed shall walk there... The wayfaring men, though fools, shall not err therein." "A city set on a hill," said our Saviour, "cannot be hid." Again: "Unless you . . . become as little children, you cannot enter into the kingdom of heaven." And again: "I thank Thee, Father, because Thou hast hid these things from the wise and prudent, and hast revealed them to little ones."

I cannot describe the relief that this thought gave to me. I saw now that my intellectual difficulties were not the real heart of the matter, and that I had no right to be discouraged because I knew myself to be immeasurably the inferior of others who had decided against the cause that was beginning to show itself to me as true. Humility and singleness of motive, I saw now, were far more important than patristic learning. I began, therefore, more than ever to aspire towards these and to throw myself upon God. I used, day after day, one of the acts of humility in St. Ignatius's *Spiritual Exercises*. In fact, I think that, owing to the violence of the reaction, I was in a certain danger of relapsing into Quietism.

But two books came to my rescue, and these were respectively Newman's *Development of Christian Doctrine* and Mallock's *Doctrine and Doctrinal Disruption*. Besides these, one of Father Carson's essays helped me in the last stage—that dealing with the growth of the Church from an embryonic condition to that of manhood; for it was, perhaps, this line of thought as much as any that especially solved my difficulties. Finally, there was Mr. Spencer Jones's *England and the Holy See*—a remarkable book, written by a man who is still a clergyman of the Church of England. These books, each in its way, helped me, not indeed directly forward towards Faith—for that was forming as independently of intellectual effort as of emotional attraction—but by way of breaking down on one side the definite difficulties that stood between me and Rome, and on the other the last remnants of theory that held me to the Church of England.

I now began to see dawning clearly, like mountains through a mist, the outlines of what I have called in the previous chapter the general or ideal views of the two Communions that claimed my allegiance. First, there was the general view of the Church of England and her relations to Christendom, and this, as I have already said, rested now entirely upon the theory of the "Church Diffusive."

Now Mr. Mallock's book first stated this theory with complete fairness and then demolished it utterly. As soon as I had finished his treatment of the question, I laid down the book and gasped. I knew, and told others that I knew, that I had no more to say on the Anglican side. There was but one hope left, and that, I thought, was impossible for me now; namely, a relapse into that kind of devout agnosticism on the subject of the Church, which is the refuge of so many Anglican clergy at the present day.

But I think now that if the other books I have mentioned had not, simultaneously, disclosed to me the outline of the Catholic Church, I should in an probability have fallen back upon that agnosticism and remained where I was, reassuring myself, as so many do, by reflections upon the tangled state of Church history and the positive evidences that God was, after all, undoubtedly working in the Anglican communion.

I need not describe at length Mr. Mallock's argument, but, in a word, it was this: the theory of the "Church Diffusive" is made by Ritualists the foundation of their belief, but the "Church Diffusive" rejects that theory; Rome, Moscow, and Canterbury, though they may agree upon other points, do not agree upon this. Therefore the authority to which the appeal is made implicitly denies that it is an authority at all. Therefore the whole thing is illusive.

I have asked, both before and since my submission to Rome, an answer to this argument and I have never yet received one of any kind. One learned and zealous Anglican could only say that it was too logical to be true, and that the heart has reasons which the head knows nothing of.

I began to turn now with more hope to the constructive books. In Mr. Spencer Jones's work I found an orderly systematization of the argument that greatly helped me to clear my thoughts; in Father Carson's essay I found a kind of brilliant variation upon Newman's great theme. But it was *The Development of Christian Doctrine* that, like a magician, waved away the last floating mists and let me see the City of God in her strength and beauty.

Finally and supremely, it was the reading of the Scriptures that satisfied me as to the positive claims of Rome. On all sides my friends told me to study the Written Word of God, and, indeed, it was the best advice that could have been given. For both I and they accepted the Scriptures as the inspired Work of God; they, in those Scriptures, interpreted by what they believed to be the Church, found the support of their own views; I, since I had lost belief in the Church to which I belonged, or rather since I failed to hear from that Church any positive interpretation at all, had nothing left but Scripture. I might read controversy for ever and fail to detect the human fallacies that might lie on either side; at least I had better turn to those writings in which confessedly there were none.

So, once more I turned to *The New Testament*, seeking to find some thread that would hold all together, some living authority to which the Scriptures themselves might point, testing, above all, the claims of that authority which on logical and human grounds seemed to me the most consistent of all claims made in Christendom—the claim of the occupier of Peter's Chair to be the Teacher and Lord of all Christians.

I have been told, of course, that I found that in *The New Testament* which I had hoped to find; that I had already accepted interiorly the claims of Rome, and therefore forced myself to the conclusion that the Scriptures must support them too. I was bidden to turn again to the theologians for the interpretation of the Scripture—back again, in fact, to that very tangle of witnesses who, on the whole, seemed to me to support the Petrine position, and whom I had, a little while ago, been advised to leave for God's own Word.

Yet what else could I do except honestly to attempt to test by that divine authority the sole claim that, alone in the whole of Christendom, seemed to me consistent, reasonable, historical, practical, satisfactory, and, from the very nature of the case, intrinsically necessary?

Well, I need not say that I found that claim there more evidently and easily than I could find many other doctrines which none the less I readily accepted on Scriptural authority. Dogmas such as that of the Blessed Trinity, sacraments such as that of Confirmation, institutions such as that of Episcopacy—all these things can indeed, to the Anglican as well as the Catholic mind, be found in Scripture if a man will dig for them. But the Petrine claim needs no digging: it lies like a great jewel, blazing on the surface, when once one has rubbed one's eyes clear of anti-Catholic predisposition.

The "One Foundation" declares that on "Cephas" He will build His Church: the Good Shepherd bids the same Cephas, even after he has forfeited, it might seem, all claims on his Lord, to "feed his sheep"; the "Door" gives to Peter the "Keys." In all I found twenty-nine passages of Scripture— since then I have found a few more—in which the Petrine prerogative is at any rate implied, and I found not one contrary to or incompatible with its commission. I published these in a small pamphlet, *A City Set on a Hill*, soon after my submission.

It is, of course, utterly impossible to lay my finger upon this or that argument as the one that finally convinced me. Besides, it was not argument that did convince me, any more than it was emotion that impelled me. It was rather my being drawn by the Spirit of God towards a vantage ground whence I could look out and see the facts as they were; but it was Newman's book that pointed me to the facts, led my eye from this point to that, and showed me how the whole glorious erection stood upon the unshakeable foundation of the Gospel and soared to heaven.

There, then, to change the metaphor, I saw the mystical Bride of Christ, growing through the ages from the state of childhood to adolescence, increasing in wisdom and stature, not adding to but developing her knowledge, strengthening her limbs, stretching out her hands; changing, indeed, her aspect and her language—using now this set of human terms, now that, to express better and better her mind; bringing out of her treasures things new and old, which yet had been hers from the beginning, indwelt by the Spirit of her Spouse, and even suffering as He had done.

She, too, was betrayed and crucified; "dying daily," like her great Lord; denied, mocked, and despised; a child of sorrows and acquainted with grief; misrepresented, misconstrued, agonizing; stripped of her garments, yet, like the King's daughter that she is, "all glorious within"; dead even, it seemed at times, yet, like her natural Prototype, still united to the Godhead; laid in the sepulchre, fenced in by secular powers, yet ever rising again on Easter Days, spiritual and transcendent; passing through doors that men thought closed for

ever, spreading her mystical banquets in upper rooms
and by sea shores; and, above all, ascending for ever
beyond the skies and dwelling in heavenly places with
Him who is her Bridegroom and her God.

Difficulty after difficulty melted as I looked on her
face. I saw now how it must be that outward aspects
should change, and that the swathed child in the
Catacombs should seem very different from the reign-
ing mother and mistress of churches, the queen of the
world. I saw, too, how even her constitution must
appear to change: how the limbs, that at first move
spasmodically and clumsily, should, as she increased in
strength, become more and more controlled by the
visible Head; how the great childish gestures of the
early Councils should pass little by little into the
serene voice issuing from the lips; how the unordered
implicit knowledge of the first centuries should express
itself more and more precisely as she learned how to
speak to men that which she knew from the beginning;
how gradually she would announce even in our own
days that principle on which she had acted from the
beginning—namely, that in matters that concerned
the vital contents of her message, she was protected, in
the utterances of her Head, by the Spirit of Truth that
had first formed her body in the womb of the human
race. For this is, in the long run, the inevitable claim
that a Church must make which professes to stand for
Revelation.

I do not say that all difficulties went at once. They
did not. In fact, I do not suppose that there is any
Catholic alive who would dare to say that he has no
difficulties even now; but "ten thousand difficulties do
not make one doubt." There remain always the old
eternal problems of sin and free will; but to one who
has once looked full into the eyes of this great Mother,
these problems are as nothing. She knows, if we do not;
she knows, even if she does not say that she knows; for

within her somewhere, far down in her great heart, there lies hid the very wisdom of God Himself.

And an this great vision I saw now *for the first time* fulfilled in what I had been accustomed to call the Church of Rome. I turned and looked again at the Church of England and there was an extraordinary change.

It was not that she had become unlovable. I love her even now as one may love an unsatisfactory human friend. She had a hundred virtues, a delicate speech, a romantic mind; a pleasant aroma hung about her; she was infinitely pathetic and appealing; she had the advantage of dwelling in the shadowed twilight of her own vagueness, in glorious houses, even though not of her building; she had certain gracious ways, pretty modes of expression; her music and her language still seem to me extraordinarily beautiful; and above all, she is the nursing mother of many of my best friends, and for over thirty years educated and nursed me, too, with indulgent kindness. Indeed, I was not ungrateful for all this, but it had become entirely impossible for me ever to reverence her again as the divine mistress of my soul.

It is true that she had fed me with the best food she had, and that Our Lord had accompanied those gifts with better gifts of His own; she had, indeed, pointed me to Him rather than to herself. But all this did not make her my queen or even my mother; and, in fact, even in other matters she had failed me, through no fault of her own, but rather because of the misfortune of her own birth and nature.

When I had asked her questions that really concerned the very life I was leading under her protection, she had given me no answer. She had told me only to lie still and love her, and that was not enough. A soul cannot be eternally satisfied with kindness and a soothing murmur and the singing of hymns, and there is a liberty which is a more intolerable slavery than the heaviest of chains. I did not want to go this way and that at my own will: I wanted to know the way in which God wished me to walk. I did not want to be free to change my grasp on truth: I needed rather a truth that itself should make me free. I did not want broad ways of pleasantness, but the narrow Way that is Truth and Life. And for all these things she was helpless.

There, then, she stood, my old mistress, pathetic and loving, claiming me as her servant by every human tie; and there, on the other side, in a blaze of fierce light, stood the Bride of Christ, dominant and imperious, but with a look in her eyes and a smile on her lips that could rise only from a heavenly vision, claiming me, not because she had as yet done anything for me, not because I was an Englishman who loved English ways—or even Italian, for the matter of that—but simply and solely because I was a child of God and because to her He had said, "Take this child away and nurse it for Me and I will give thee thy wages"; because, first and last, she was His Bride and I was His son.

If at that choice I had hesitated and turned back to her whom I knew and loved) in preference to her whom as yet I saw and feared only at a distance, I know that I should have fallen, without even the shadow of a doubt, under that condemnation uttered by my Lord: "Unless a man leave his father and mother and all that he hath, he cannot be My disciple." I went to my Superior, therefore, in the early summer, told him once more of my state of mind, and obtained leave from him to go home to my mother's house for a few months' rest and reflection.

Tremans

CHAPTER SIX

I WAS in a very curious and unsatisfactory state when I came home. I do not propose to discuss these symptoms in public, but, to sum it up in a word, I was entirely exhausted on the spiritual side. Yet it was now absolutely clear to me, so far as I could see intellectually, that my submission was a duty. I made this clear also to my mother, from whom I had had no secrets from the beginning; and I settled down, as she desired me, towards, I think, the end of May, to allow myself time and energy for a reaction, if such should come.

Occasionally I celebrated the Communion still in the little chapel of the house, for the reasons that I have already explained; but, with the consent of my Superior, I refused all invitations to preach, saying that my plans were at present undecided. This, of course, was absolutely true, as I sufficiently trusted my Superior's and my mother's judgment to allow of the possibility of a change of mind. I was still technically a member of the Community of the Resurrection, said my Office regularly, and observed the other details of the rule that were binding upon me. I had told, however, a few intimate friends of what I thought would happen.

I have mentioned before a certain MS. book upon the Elizabethan days of the Church of England. This had aroused my interest, and I began to consider whether, as a kind of safety-valve, I could not make some sort of historical novel upon the subject. The result was that I was soon hard at work upon a book, afterwards published under the title, *By What Authority?* It was extraordinary how excited I became. I worked for about eight or ten hours every day, either writing, or reading and annotating every historical book and pamphlet I could lay my hands upon. I found paragraphs in magazines, single sentences in certain essays, and all of these I somehow worked into the material from which my book grew.

By the beginning of September the novel was three-quarters finished. I have formed a great many criticisms upon that book now. It is far too long; it is rather sentimental; it is too full of historical detail; above all, the mental atmosphere there depicted is at least a century before its time; men did not, until almost Caroline days, think and feel as I have represented them thinking and feeling in Elizabeth's reign. In two points only am I satisfied with it: there is, I think, a certain pleasant freshness about it, and I have not as yet detected in it any historical errors. I was absurdly careful in details that were wholly negligible with regard to general historical truth. This work, I think, was an exceptionally good safety-valve, for my spirits, and if I had not found it I do not quite know what would have happened.

Now, more than ever, my resolution began to run clear. In book after book that I read I found the old lines of the Church of England burning themselves upwards, like the lines of buried foundations showing through the grass in a hot summer. I began to marvel more than ever how in the world I could have even imagined that the Anglican Communion possessed an identity of life with the ancient Church in England.

For years past I had claimed to be saying Mass, and that the Sacrifice of the Mass was held as a doctrine by the Church of England; and here in Elizabethan days were priests hunted to death for the crime of doing that which I had claimed to do. I had supposed that our wooden Communion tables were altars, and here in Tudor times were the old stones of the altars defiled and insulted deliberately by the officials of the Church to which I still nominally belonged, and wooden tables substituted instead. Things which were dear to me at Mirfield—vestments, crucifixes, rosaries—in Elizabethan days were denounced as "trinkets" and "muniments of superstition." I began to wonder at myself, and a little while later gave up celebrating the Communion service.

Sometime in the course of the summer, at my mother's wish, I went to consult three eminent members of the Church of England—a well known parish clergyman, an eminent dignitary, and a no less eminent layman. They were all three as kind as possible. Above all, not one of them reproached me with disloyalty to my father's memory. They understood, as all with chivalrous instincts must have understood, that such an argument as that was wholly unworthy.

The parish clergyman did not affect me at all. He hardly argued, and he said very little that I can remember, except to call attention to the revival of spiritual life in the Church of England during the last century. I did not see that this proved anything except that God rewarded an increase of zeal by an increase of blessing. He himself was an excellent example of both. Neither could I see the force of his further argument that, since this spiritual revival showed itself along sacramental lines, therefore here was an evidence for the validity of

Anglican Sacraments. For, first, precisely the same revival has been at work with regard to sacramental views among the Presbyterians, and high-church Anglicans do not for that reason accept the validity of Presbyterian Orders; and, second, it is natural that among Anglicans the revival should have taken that form, since *The Prayer Book* itself affords scope in this direction.

The dignitary with whom I stayed a day or two, and who was also extremely forbearing, did not, I think, understand my position. He asked me whether there were not devotions in the Roman Church to which I felt a repugnance. I told him that there were—notably the popular devotions to Our Blessed Lady. He then expressed great surprise that I could seriously contemplate submitting to a communion in which I should have to use methods of worship of which I disapproved.

I tried in vain to make it clear that I proposed becoming a Roman Catholic not because I was necessarily attracted by her customs, but because I believed that Church to be the Church of God, and that therefore if my opinions on minor details differed from hers, it was all the worse for me; that I had better, in fact, correct my notions as soon as possible, for I should go to Rome not as a critic or a teacher, but as a child and a learner. I think he thought this an immoral point of view. Religion seemed to him to be a matter more or less of individual choice and tastes.

This interview afforded me one more illustration of the conviction which I had formed to the effect that as a Teaching Body—as fulfilling, that is, the principal function for which Christ instituted a Church—the Church of England was hopeless. Here was one of her chief rulers assuming, almost as an axiom, that I must accept only those dogmas that individually happened to recommend themselves to my reason or my temperament. Tacitly, then, he allowed no authoritative power on the part of the Church to demand an intellectual submission; tacitly, again, then, he made no real distinction between Natural and Revealed Religion: Christ had not revealed positive truths to which, so soon as we accepted Christ as a Divine Teacher, we instantly submitted without hesitation. Or, if this seem too strong, it may be said that the prelate in question at any rate denied the existence anywhere on earth of an authority capable of proposing the truths of Revelation in an authoritative manner, and hence, indirectly evacuated Revelation of any claim to demand man's submission.

The layman, with whom also I stayed, had showed me many kindnesses before, and now crowned them all by his charity and sympathy. He emphasized the issues with extreme clearness, telling me that if I believed the Pope to be the necessary centre of Christian unity, of course I must submit to him at once; but he asked me to be quite certain that this was so. and not to submit merely because I thought the Pope an extremely useful aid to unity. The layman further told me that he himself believed that the Pope was the natural outcome of ecclesiastical development; that he was Vicar of Christ *jure ecclesiastico*, but not *jure divino*; and he pointed out to me that, unless I was absolutely certain of the latter point, I should be far happier in the Church of England and far more useful in the work of promoting Christian unity. With all this I heartily agreed.

A further curious circumstance was that, at this time, a prelate was staying in the house with me who had had a great influence upon my previous life. He knew why I was there, but I do not think we spoke of it at all. After my return home again, my late host sent me a quantity of extraordinarily interesting private documents, which I read and returned. But they did not affect me. They are documents that have since been published.

Towards the end of July I was once more tired out in mind and soul, and was in further misery because an ultimatum had come from Mirfield, perfectly kind and perfectly firm, telling me that I must now either return to the annual assembling of the community or consider myself no longer a member. The Brother who was commissioned to write this had been a fellow-probationer of mine, with whom I had been on terms of great intimacy. He wrote in obvious distress, and after my answer, written in equal distress, telling him that I could not come back, I never since received any communication from him until one day when I met him by chance in the train. We took up then, I hoped at the time, our old friendship; but even more recently he has again refused my acquaintance, on the ground that I showed too much "bitterness" in public controversy.

Further, about this time I was engaged in an other rather painful correspondence. A dignitary of the Church of England, the occupant of an historic see and an old friend of my family, hearing somehow that I was in distress of mind as to my spiritual allegiance, wrote to me an extremely kind letter, asking me to come and stay with him. I answered that I was indeed in trouble, but had already looked into the matter so far as I was capable. But I suppose that I must have seemed to hint that I was still open to conviction, for he wrote again, still more affectionately, and then somehow the correspondence became the retraversing of the old ground I had passed months before.

Finally I told him plainly that I was already intellectually decided, and received in answer a very sharp letter or two, telling me that if I would only go and work hard in some slum parish all my difficulties would disappear. He might equally well have told me to go and teach Buddhism. In his last letter he prophesied that one of three things would happen to me: either (which he hoped) I should return quickly to the Church of

England with my sanity regained, or (which he feared)
I should lose my Christian belief altogether, or (which
he seemed to fear still more, and in which he was
perfectly right) I should become an obstinate, hardened
Romanist. It appeared to him impossible that faith and
open-mindedness should survive conversion. I hope I
have not wronged him in this representation of his
views. I destroyed his letter immediately.

In order to distract myself from all this, I then went
for a few days' bicycling tour alone in the south of
England, dressed as a layman, calling first at the
Carthusian Monastery of St. Hugh, Parkminster, with
an introduction to one of the Fathers, himself a convert clergyman. He received me very courteously, but
the visit depressed me even further, if that were possible. He seemed to me not to understand that I really
asked nothing but to be taught; that I was not coming
as a critic, but as a child. I do not think that I resented
this, because my whole soul told me it was not quite
just; if it had been just, I think I should have assumed
a kind of internal indignation as a salve to wounded
vanity.

I went on in despair and stayed a Sunday in lodg-
ings at Chichester, where for the last time, in a little
church opposite the Cathedral, I made my Anglican
Confession, telling the clergyman plainly that I was
practically certain I should become a Roman Catholic.
He very kindly gave me his absolution and told me to
cheer up.

Then for the last time I attended, as an Anglican,
cathedral services and received Communion; for I still
thought it my duty to use every conceivable means of
grace within my reach. On the Monday I rode on to
Lewes, thence to Rye, where, at supper in the "George
Inn," I had a long conversation with a man whom I
took to be a certain distinguished actor, talking to him
for the most part about the Catholic Church, which he

also loved from a distance, but not saying anything about my intentions. As a matter of fact, he did nearly all the talking.

On the following day I rode home by Mayfield, all through a blazing summer's day, looking with a kind of gnawing envy at the convent walls as I passed them, and staying for a few minutes in a beautiful little dark Catholic Church that I ran across unexpectedly in a valley.

Now it seems very difficult to say why I had not submitted before this. The reasons, I think, were as follows. First, there was the wish of my mother and family that I should allow myself every possible opportunity for a change of mind under new surroundings, and this, even, by itself, would have been sufficient to hold me back for a while. I was trying to be docile, it must be remembered, and to take every hint that could possibly come from God.

Secondly, there was my own state of mind, which, though intellectually convinced, was still in an extraordinary condition. I entirely refuse to describe it elaborately—it would not be decent; but the sum of it was a sense of a huge, soulless, spiritual wilderness, in which, as clear as a view before rain, towered up the City of God. It was there before me, as vivid and overwhelming as a revelation, and I stood there and eyed it, watching for the least wavering if it were a mirage, or the least hint of evil if it were of the devil's building. Cardinal Newman's phrase describes best, I think, my mental condition. I knew that the Catholic Church was the true Church, but I did not absolutely know that I knew it.

I had no kind of emotional attraction towards it, no illusions of any kind about it. I knew perfectly well that it was human as well as divine, that crimes had been committed within its walls; that the ways and customs and language of its citizens would be other than those of the dear homely town which I had left; that I should find hardness there, unfamiliar manners, even suspicion and blame.

But for all that it was divine; it was built upon the Rock of rocks; its foundations were jewelled even if its streets were as hard as gold; and the Lamb was the light of it.

But the setting out towards its gates was a hard task. I had no energy, no sense of welcome or exultation; I knew hardly more than three or four of its inmates. I was deadly sick and tired of the whole thing.

But God was merciful very soon. Even now I do not exactly know what precipitated the final step; the whole world seemed to me poised in a kind of paralysis... I could not move; there was no other to suggest it to me... But at the beginning of September, with my mother's knowledge, I wrote a letter to a priest I knew personally, putting myself in his hands. This friend of mine, also a convert, was now contemplating entering the Dominican Order, and recommended me, therefore, to Father Reginald Buckler, O.P., then living at Woodchester. Two or three days later I received notice that I was expected at the Priory, and on Monday, September 7, in lay clothes, I set out on my journey. My mother said good-bye to me at the station.

near
Woodchester

CHAPTER SEVEN

I DO NOT suppose that anyone ever entered the City of God with less emotion than mine. It seemed to me that I was utterly without feeling; I had neither joy nor sorrow, nor dread nor excitement. There was the Truth, as aloof as an ice peak, and I had to embrace it. Never for one single instant did I doubt that, nor, perhaps it is unnecessary to say, have I ever doubted it since. I tried to reproach myself with my coldness, but all fell quite flat. I was as one coming out of the glare of artificial light, out of warmth and brightness and friendliness, into a pale daylight of cold and dreary certainty. I was uninterested and quite positive.

I arrived at Stroud towards evening, saying my Anglican Office for the last time on the way, and, after waiting about for a while, entered the omnibus for Woodchester, which is a few miles distant.

The drive was as dreary as everything else, though it should not have been, for the country is really beautiful and romantic. There is a long twisting valley between hills that rise on either side in a manner not unlike some parts of Italy. We drove on and on; I listened unintelligently to the conversation of an old man with a rosy face, and noticed one or two children who were troublesome. But nothing seemed to me to matter at all or to be of the slightest significance.

A lay-brother was waiting for me at the foot of the little steep stony path that leads from the road to the Priory, and together we climbed it. Near the gate of the church, in the darkening evening light, there was standing a figure in white, who, when he saw us, came down the hill and took my hands in his; and, almost in silence, we went on and into the house. But even then I was utterly dull and stupid.

I do not propose to describe in detail the three days that followed. After all, I do not know why anyone should be interested in them. Nor do I propose to describe the endless kindness, courtesy, and patience that I found in Father Reginald and the Prior, and, in fact, in everyone with whom I had to do.

My instructor and I walked together on the three afternoons and talked of this and that, and in my spare time I studied *The Penny Catechism*. One detail, however, I must mention, at the risk even of annoying that dear Dominican Father. He asked me on the Thursday whether I had any difficulties. I told him "No." "But, surely, indulgences!" he said. Again I told him that these were not the slightest difficulty. I was not sure that I perfectly understood them, but I was quite sure that I perfectly believed them, as indeed everything else which the Church proposed to my faith. But he was not quite satisfied, and gave me a full and detailed instruction on the point.

On these evenings, too, he always came in for an hour or two in my room, on the first floor. Each morning I heard Mass and attempted a sort of meditation. I attended other Offices now and then and was always at Compline and the exquisite Dominican ceremony of the *Salve Regina* afterwards. I noticed also with mild interest the resemblance of the Dominican to the Sarum rite in various points.

On the Friday, the day fixed for my reception, I took a long, lonely walk, still entirely uninterested, and visited the church of Minchinhampton, on the opposite side of the valley. I was caught in the rain, I remember, and had tea in a small public-house parlour, where there was a rather witty list of instructions to visitors as to the personal prowess of the landlord and his intentions of enforcing order. Then I came back to the Priory about six o'clock.

I cannot imagine why I am writing down all this, except that it seems impossible to think of the events of those days under any other images than those of the small external details which happened. Even if I had glowing spiritual experiences to record, I should not do so; but the truth is that I had none. There seemed nothing within me at all except an absolute certainty that I was doing God's will and was entering the doors of His Church. I had no elevations of spirit and no temptations against faith or anything else; and this, I must confess, lasted not only through my reception and First Communion, but for some months afterwards. Even Rome itself, though I learned strange and astounding lessons there, sent very few emotions through me.

In fact, I was experiencing at this time the natural reaction of the very real and appalling struggle that I had been engaged in previously for nearly a year. During that time, in various forms, I had gone through the whole gamut of such spiritual life as I possessed, and the result was that my faculties had sunk into a kind of lethargy. Even this I only mention now, as I have known more than one convert utterly dismayed and astonished at similar experiences. The soul had expected the visible opening of heaven, the pouring out of floods of sensible grace, torrents of pleasure, dazzling glory and super-terrestrial sounds, and instead there had descended a pall of heaviness with but one light to pierce it, and that the Star of Divine Faith, as steady and certain as God upon His throne.

Of course those souls are very happy who find it otherwise. One such friend of mine, now a priest also, told me that his supreme difficulty in making his submission was the thought that he must repudiate his own Orders. Up to that time he had been a Ritualistic clergyman, doing a devoted work among the poor in one of the great English towns and celebrating every day for years what he believed to be the Holy Sacrifice of the Mass.

He told me that he almost dreaded his First Communion, because he was afraid that, since it was inconceivable that Our Lord could be more gracious to him than He had been at Anglican altars, he himself might be tempted to doubt the reality of the change. But the moment that the Sacred Host touched his tongue he knew the difference. He told me that never again after that moment did he doubt for a single second that hitherto he had received nothing but bread and wine, accompanied by unsacramental grace, and that this new gift was indeed nothing else than the Immaculate Body of Christ. He is, moreover, a middle-aged, unemotional man.

At about half-past six Father Reginald took me into the Chapter House, and there, kneeling down by the Prior's seat, I made my confession, together with acts of faith, hope, charity, and contrition, and received absolution. I did not receive conditional baptism—although of course I was perfectly willing to do so—since two witnesses at my previous baptism had given independent testimony that the ceremony had been undoubtedly performed according to Catholic requirements. Then, like a father with his son, he kissed me, and I went through into church to make my thanksgiving.

On the following morning I received Holy Communion in the beautiful little church, from the hands of the Prior. I stayed over the Sunday, with a curious, passionless kind of contentment growing in my heart almost every moment, and on the Monday journeyed up to the north to stay with my priest-friend, who was then acting as chaplain to a Catholic household.

Rather a strange surprise awaited me here. A few weeks previously I had had one of those vivid dreams that leave, during all the day that follows them, an inexplicable, incommunicable joy. I had dreamed that I was walking alone over high hills towards the sea, feeling rather lonely and desolate. The ground was bare all about me, but as I went on I began to see woods in front, and then suddenly I came out on a hilltop and saw below me a great sweep of woods and beyond them the sea. But set right in the middle of the woods was the roof of a large house, and the moment I saw this I was conscious of a sudden overwhelming joy, as of a child coming home. Then I awoke, still extraordinarily happy.

Now I had never before been to see my friend, nor had he ever given me the least outline of a description of the place in which he lived. I did not even know that it was near the sea. When, therefore, I arrived and saw that the sea was not far off, I was interested, and told my friend the dream, remarking that in other points there was no resemblance between the dream and this place.

But on the next morning he took me up a hill behind the house, and there, strangely enough, in all their main features the two things corresponded. There were the roofs and chimneys of the Catholic house, the sweep of the woods, and the long horizon of the sea beyond. Yet there were one or two small details, which I now forget, which appeared to me different; neither was there any emotional sense of joy.

And now began the inevitable consequences of what I had done. I do not know how many letters I received in the few days following the announcement in the papers of my conversion; but I had at least two heavy posts every day. These had to be answered, and what made it harder was that among them all there were not more than two or three from Catholics. This was perfectly natural, as I hardly knew more than that number of Catholics. One telegram indeed warmed my heart; for it was from that priest to whom I owed so much and of whose conversion I had heard with such sorrow in Damascus six years before.

The rest were from Anglicans—clergy, men, women, and even children—most of whom regarded me either as a deliberate traitor (but of these there were very few) or as an infatuated fool, or as an impatient, headstrong, ungrateful bigot. Many of these kindly concealed their sentiments as well as they could, but it was for the most part plain enough what they thought. From one clergyman, still an Anglican, I received an enthusiastic letter of congratulation on having been happy enough to have found my way into the City of Peace. Eight years later he also entered that city.

I think that I answered them all, even down to one from a sincere woman who besought me to remember a sermon I had once preached upon the Prodigal Son, and to make haste to come back to the Father's house. I answered this, very naturally, by observing that, on the contrary, I had just done so, pointing out to her that no conceivable motive except the conviction to that effect would have brought me out of the Church of England. I also expressed a hope that one day she would come too. She handed my letter to her clergyman, who replied to me instantly with a violent accusation of treachery, telling me that when he had asked me to preach a mission in his parish he had thought me to be trustworthy; he was sorry now that my "perversion" had so quickly degraded my character. Again I answered by quoting his parishioner's remarks to me and observing that I could scarcely answer her otherwise than the way in which I had done. He replied once more with a half-apology, saying that the woman had given him to understand that I had written to her first, and that he regretted having used such strong expressions.

Another letter which I received caused me considerable pain as well as astonishment. It was from a middle-aged woman whom I had thought sincerely my friend—the wife of an eminent dignitary in the Church of England. The letter was short, bitter, and fierce, reproaching me for the dishonour I had done to my father's name and memory. It seemed to me then—and it seems to me still —incomprehensible that a person of true and deep religion, such as she undoubtedly was, should utter this particular reproach; just as if the thought of this dishonour to my father had not been so evidently a Satanic temptation that I had not dared even to hesitate over its rejection. Very different from this was the deep and generous phrase of a certain Anglican Bishop, who, in speaking to my mother after my departure for Rome, said to her, "Remember that he has followed his conscience after all, and what else could his father wish for him than that?" I can only conclude that the letter was written in a mood of blind anger.

But such controversies were very rare. Once again, later, I was informed by a clergyman that such an act of schism as I had committed always bore "bitter fruit," and that apparently in my case, as in so many others, "honour had taken to itself wings." All this was apropos of the fact that after my ordination in Rome I had come harmlessly to live in the same town as himself, though not engaged at that time in any evangelistic works, and that nearly two years previously, against my own will, I had been sent to preach an Anglican mission in his parish. I answered by hinting that unless he withdrew those expressions, which I knew very well he would repeat in private conversations, I should consider myself at liberty to send his letter to the newspapers. He withdrew them.

Yet, with a very few exceptions of this kind, I must acknowledge with the greatest gratitude that the charity with which I was treated by members of the Anglican communion in general simply astonished me. I did not know that there was so much generosity in the world.

A few days later I went to stay at Erdington Abbey, with the Benedictines, and here again I began to find more and more evidences of the welcome that was waiting for me in my true home. Two of the Fathers, themselves convert-clergymen, took all pains to set me at my ease and to show me kindness and sympathy in every conceivable way. It was reassuring to me also at this time to meet here another well-known clergyman, of whom previously I had known nothing except by reputation, and who had preceded me by a few months into the Catholic Church. I need not say that we talked a great deal.

A day or two later, once more I went back to my mother's house, where I had the satisfaction of finishing the last pages of *By What Authority?* before leaving England, on All Souls' Day, to take up my residence in Rome with a view to studying for the priesthood.

One more instance of Anglican charity occurred two minutes after my train had left Victoria station. As my mother was turning away, she saw coming towards her a prelate of the Episcopalian Scottish Church, a High Churchman and an old friend of her own. He had come to say good-bye to me and to wish me God-speed. I have not forgotten that and, please God, I never shall.

St Winefride

S. Maria Maggiore, Rome

CHAPTER EIGHT

AND now I do not know whether it is respectful to my holy mother the Church to attempt to say what she has been to me ever since the day that I walked blind and dumb and miserable into her arms. But I have said so much of others that I will venture even this. She, too, needs no charity of mine, for she is the fount and river of it.

It seems very remarkable to be obliged to say that the idea of returning to the Church of England is as inconceivable as the idea of seeking to enter the Choctaw fold. Yet, humanly speaking, and looking at it from the Anglican side, so far as that is possible, I quite understand why it is that Anglicans are always accustomed to say of every convert that "he is certain to come back." First of all, they naturally desire that all persons, however obscure, who are not likely to disgrace themselves, should be under the same allegiance as that to which they pay their own homage. Why, Catholics have a similar wish on their side!

Secondly, in a word, they do not understand the situation. They are so accustomed to division and disunion on the deepest matters of faith in their own body, that they can scarcely conceive its being otherwise elsewhere. Either, they say, these divisions must be in Catholicism too, though beneath the surface, or, if they are not, it must mean that intellectual activity is suppressed by the "iron uniformity" of the system. They do not at all understand how "the truth can make (us) free." It is a complete begging of the question, I allow, but it appears to me more true every day that I live, that those few persons who do return do so either by the road of complete unbelief, or through some grave sin in their lives, or through a species of insanity, or through the fact that they never really grasped the Catholic position at all.

It is of no use to pile up asseverations, but, in word, it may be said that to return from the Catholic Church to the Anglican would be the exchange of certitude for doubt, of faith for agnosticism, of substance for shadow, of brilliant light for sombre gloom, of historical, worldwide fact for unhistorical, provincial theory.

I do not know how to express myself more mildly than that; though even this, no doubt, will appear a monstrous extravagance, at the least, to the sincere and whole-hearted members of the Anglican communion. Only yesterday, in fact, an educated young High Churchman looked me unblenchingly in the face and said that the "Roman idea is all very well in theory; but as a practical system it does not work —it does not square with history; whereas the Anglican communion...—" Well, well!

Are there, then, no defects or disappointments that await the convert to Catholicism? There are as many defects awaiting his discovery as reside in human nature; the number of his disappointments will vary according to the number of his expectations.

First, then, there is a very singular attitude assumed by many Catholics, whose own faith is beyond doubt, with regard to the conversion of non-Catholics, and of the English in particular. I omit as irrelevant, of course, the lukewarmness of the lukewarm, or the actual religious spite of the very few persons who are actually jealous of others possessing what they themselves find so precious. It is rather of the strange mentality of persons who, themselves practising their faith fervently, seem entirely indifferent to the missionary duties of the Church. "I hear that A. B. has become a Catholic," said a good Catholic woman once. "What in the world has she done that for?"

Now such an attitude of mind as this is not only a defect—to use a very mild word—but it was, for me at any rate, a very real disappointment. It had never even entered my head to expect that such a position could be conceivable in one who valued his faith. And, to tell the truth, it is not so uncommon as one might think. Now this is nothing else than sheer Sectarianism; for unless the Catholic Religion is intended for the whole world, it is false. It is literally Catholic, or nothing.

Well, this was completely bewildering to me. I had been taught to believe that Catholics had at least the grace of Proselytism; that they possessed, at any rate, that passion for converting others which is usually one of the signs of strong conviction. And here I found, not only indifference in many cases, but even a kind of veiled opposition towards every form of activity in this direction. "Converts have so much zeal," it is said; "they are indiscreet and impetuous. The steady old ways are preferable; let us keep our faith to ourselves, and let others keep theirs."

I have come lately to understand that this Sectarianism is perhaps in some cases the result of the centuries of penal law under which Catholics in England have lived. They have been for so long accustomed to shroud their sacred mysteries, in order to protect both the mysteries and themselves, that a kind of formless tradition has grown up to the effect that it is best to leave well alone and to risk as little as possible. If that is so, Sectarianism is at least an honourable scar; yet it is none the less a defect. Curiously enough, however, it is not usually among the really old Catholic families that it makes its appearance; these are, generally, as ardent missionaries as the convert himself: it is rather among the spiritually nouveaux riches—among the Catholics of one or two generations only—that this spiritual snobbishness is the more frequent.

A second defect, akin to the first, is that of jealousy against converts. Now I should not have ventured to draw particular attention to this if I myself had suffered from it to any marked degree, since in that case I should distrust my own judgment in dealing with it. The fact is that I have not. I have received extraordinary generosity on all sides, even in such matters as my very early ordination in Rome after only nine months of Catholic life. Of course there were many who disapproved of the rapidity with which I was promoted to the priesthood, but in practically all these cases it would be ludicrously impossible to suspect in them the presence of jealousy or of that subtle form of it which manifests itself in a desire to snub the neophyte. On the whole I am astonished at the kindness which Catholics have always shown to me.

But I have come across case after case, have heard sentences and fragments of conversation which leave no possibility for doubting but that many converts do find jealousy and suspicion on the part of second-rate Catholics as among the greatest trials of their life. Such an attitude is, indeed, exceedingly human and natural. "Thou hast made them equal unto us," cries the man in the parable, "who have borne the burden and heat of the day!" And this attitude is, of course, often apparently justified by the ill-behaviour and the arrogance of a convert or two now and then—of persons who march into the Church, so to speak, with banners flying and drums playing, as if they themselves were the conquerors instead of the conquered.

But, honestly, I think that arrogance amongst converts is extremely rare. The course of instruction through which they have to pass, the vast sacrifices which many of them have had to make—these things, to say nothing of the amazing Grace of God that has brought them into the Church at all, usually purge and chasten the soul in an extraordinary degree. After all, *ceteris paribus*, the convert has been called upon by God to give a greater witness of sincerity than can any man, who, as a Catholic from the cradle, has found his main duty merely in the keeping of the Faith. *Ceteris paribus*, it is a more heroic act to break with the past than to be loyal to it.

Here, again, however, it is not amongst the genuine "old Catholics"—the aristocrats of the Faith, so to speak—that jealousy or suspicion towards converts usually manifest themselves, but, once more, amongst those who desire to be thought so—amongst those who, in a determination to mark their aloofness from the "convert-spirit," think to advertise the fact by fault-finding and ill-mannered contempt. They have come into their fortune comparatively recently, and they think to hide their spiritual origins by snubbing those who make no claim to such spiritual aristocracy. It is among this class, too, that that other kind of jealousy on behalf of favourite churches or priests usually manifests itself—a jealousy that is not content with plaguing the life out of the unhappy clergy, who, they think, alone can understand them, but proceeds further by slander and spite and gossip to attack the good name of everyone else.

There are, then, defects amongst Catholics—I have named two—and it is entirely useless to deny them.

Only they are not, in the very least, of the kind which non-Catholics suspect or pretend. These defects are such as are common to human nature everywhere—to individuals, that is, who fail to live up to the standards of their religion. But the faults supposed by Anglicans to be most characteristic of those who pay their allegiance to Rome are simply not characteristic at all.

First, there is absolutely none of that diversity on matters of faith which the Anglican, in his own case, apparently accepts as his "cross"; there are no "schools of thought" in this sense, at all; there is not the faintest dogmatic difference between these two groups of temperaments into which the whole human race may more or less be divided—the maximizers and the minimizers—or, as they are labelled by Anglicans in the case of the Catholic Church—the Ultramontanes and the Gallicans. So far as these camps exist at all, though, frankly, I must confess my entire inability so to classify Catholics, they are concerned, I imagine, merely with the prudence or imprudence of a proposed action, with a like or dislike of "Roman" methods and such like secondary affairs.

Again, there is no "seething discontent," so far as I am aware, within the walls of the Church. Certainly I continually am hearing of it, but always from non-Catholics. There is no intellectual revolt on the part of the stronger minds of the Roman communion that I have ever heard of—except from non-Catholics. There is no "alienation of the men"; on the contrary, in this country, as also in Italy and France, I am continually astonished by the extraordinary predominance of the male sex over the female in attendance at Mass and in the practice of private prayer in our churches. At a recent casual occasion, upon my remarking to the parish-priest of a suburban church that I have always been struck by this phenomenon, he told me that on the previous evening he had happened to count the

congregation from the west gallery and that the pro-
portion of men to women had been about as two to one.
This, of course, was something of an exceptional illustration of my point.

All these charges, therefore, so freely levelled
against us, are, it appears to me, entirely void of
substance. Of course there are hot temperaments and
cold, apostolic and diplomatic natures, among Catholics, as elsewhere.

Of course occasionally a little revolt breaks out, as
it will break out in every human society; of course self-
willed persons—women as well as men —will occasionally dissociate themselves from Catholic life, or,
worse still, attempt to remain Catholic in name while
wholly un-Catholic in spirit. But what I mean to deny
is that these incidents even approximate to tendencies—still less that, as tendencies, they are in the
faintest degree characteristic of Catholicism—or that
the astonishing calm on the surface of the Church is,
as a matter of fact, undermined by fierce internal
struggles. It is simply not true.

Again, I must emphatically deny that formalism is
characteristic of Catholicism in a way that it is not
characteristic of Protestantism. There is, however,
just this shadow of truth in the charge; viz., that
amongst Catholics emotionalism and even strong sen-
timent is considerably discouraged, and that the heart
of religion is thought rather to reside in the adherence
and obedience of the will. The result is, of course, that
persons of a comparatively undevout nature will, as
Catholics, continue to practise their religion, and
sometimes, in ungenerous characters, only the barest
minimum of their obligations; whereas as Anglicans
they would give it up altogether.

It follows that perhaps it may be true to say that the
average emotional level of a Catholic congregation is
lower than the corresponding level of a Protestant

congregation, but it is not at an a consequence that
therefore Catholics are more formalistic than Protestants. These cold, undevout souls—or rather these
souls of a naturally undevout temperament—adhere to
their religion through the sheer motive of obedience,
and it is surely remarkable to condemn them on that
account! Obedience to the will of God—or even what
is merely believed to be the will of God—is actually
more meritorious, not less, when it is unaccompanied
by emotional consolations and sensible fervour.

In a word, then, I would say this: that, judging from
an experience of nine years as an Anglican clergyman
and eight years as a Catholic priest, there are defects in
both the Catholic and the Anglican communions; that
in the case of the Anglican these defects are vital and
radical, since they are flaws in what ought to be divinely intact—flaws, that is to say, in such things as
the certitude of faith, the unity of believers, and the
authority of those who should be teachers in the Name
of God; and that in the case of the Catholic Church
the flaws are merely those of flawed humanity, inseparable from the state of imperfection in which all men
are placed. The flaws of Anglicanism, and indeed in
Protestantism generally, are evidences that the system
is not divine; the flaws in the Catholic system show no
more than that it has a human side as well as a divine,
and this no Catholic has ever dreamed of denying.

In Rome I learned one supremely large lesson,
among a hundred others. It has been very well said that
Gothic architecture represents the soul aspiring to
God, and that Renaissance or Romanesque architecture represents God tabernacling with men. Both sides
are true, yet neither, in the religion of the Incarnation,
is complete without the other.

On the one side, it is true that the soul must always
be seeking, always gazing up through the darkness to a
God who hides Himself, always remembering that the

Infinite transcends the finite and that an immense agnosticism must be an element in every creed; the lines of this world, as it were, run up into gloom; the light that glimmers through carved tracery and heavy stains is enough to walk by, but little more. It is in silence that God is known, and through mysteries that He declares Himself. "God is a spirit," formless, infinite, invisible, and eternal, and "they that worship Him must worship Him in spirit and in truth." Here, then, is mysticism and the darkness of spiritual experience.

Then, on the other side, God became man—"the Word was made flesh." The divine, unknowable Nature struck itself into flesh and "tabernacled amongst us, and we beheld His glory." What was hidden was made known. It is not only we who thirst and knock: it is God Who, thirsting for our love, died upon the cross that He might open the kingdom of heaven to all believers, Who rent the veil of the Temple by His death-groan, and Who still stands knocking at every human heart, that He may come in and sup with man. The round dome of heaven is brought down to earth; the walls of the world are plain to the sight; its limitations are seen in the light of God; the broad sunshine of Revelation streams on all sides through clear windows upon a gorgeous pavement; angels and gods and men riot together in an intoxication of divine love; the high altar stands plain to view in a blaze of gilding and candles; and above it the round brazen and silken tent of God-made-man stands that all alike may see and adore.

Now, this side of the religion of the Incarnation had hitherto meant almost nothing to me. I was a Northerner pure and simple, educated in Northern ways. I loved twilight and mysterious music and the shadow of deep woods; I hated open spaces of sun and trumpets in unison and the round and square in architecture. I preferred meditation to vocal prayer, Mme. Guyon to Mother Julian, *John Inglesant* to St. Thomas, the thirteenth century— as I imagined it—to the sixteenth.

Until towards the end of my Anglican life I should frankly have acknowledged this; then I should have resented the accusation, for I was beginning to understand— and, therefore, thought that I entirely understood —that the world was as material as it was spiritual, and that creeds were as necessary as aspirations. But when I came to Rome I acknowledged to myself once more how little I had understood.

Here was this city, Renaissance from end to end, yet under clear skies and a burning sun; and the religion in it was the soul dwelling in the body. It was the assertion of the reality of the human principle as embodying the divine. Even the exclusive tenets of Christianity were expressed under pagan images. Revelation spoke through forms of natural religion; God dwelt unashamed in the light of day; priests were priests, not aspiring clergymen; they sacrificed, sprinkled lustral water, went in long, rolling processions with incense and lights, and called heaven Olympus. *Sacrum Divo Sebastiano*, I saw inscribed on a granite altar.

I sat under priest-professors who shouted, laughed, and joyously demonstrated before six nations in one lecture room. I saw the picture of the "Father of princes and kings and Lord of the world" exposed in the streets on his name-day, surrounded by flowers and oil lamps, in the manner in which, two centuries ago, other lords of the world were honoured. I went down into the Catacombs on St. Cecilia's Day and St. Valentine's, and smelled the box and the myrtle underfoot that did reverence to the fragrance of their memories, as centuries ago they had done reverence to victors in another kind of contest. In one sentence, I began to understand that "the Word was made flesh and dwelt among us"; that as He took the created substance of a Virgin to

fashion for Himself a natural body, so still He takes the
created substance of men—their thoughts, their expressions, and their methods—to make for Himself
that mystical body by which He is with us always; in
short, I perceived that "there is nothing secular but
sin." Catholicism, then, is "materialistic?" Certainly;
it is as materialistic as the Creation and the Incarnation, neither more nor less.

It is impossible to describe what this discovery
means to a Northern soul. Certainly it means the
obscuring of some of the old lights that had once
seemed so beautiful in the half-gloom of individual
experience, or rather, their drowning in the strong
sunshine. Set beside some Roman pomp an exquisite
Anglican service: how provincial, domestic, and indi-
vidualistic becomes the latter! Set beside a Gregorian
professor lecturing to Greeks, Roumanians, and
Frenchmen, on the principles of restitution or the duty
of citizens to the State, an Anglican divine expound-
ing St. Paul's Epistles to theological students; a friar in
S. Carlo beside the most passionate mission preacher
in the Church of England; the olive-laden peasants
shouting hymns in S. Giovanne in Laterano beside a
devout company of Anglicans gathered for Evensong;
an hieratic sacrificer in S. Maria Maggiore beside the
most perfectly drilled Ritualist in Mass vestments !

Oh! Set any section of Catholic faith and worship
seen in holy Rome beside the corresponding section of
Anglican faith and worship! Yet Anglicans are shocked
in Rome, and Dissenters exclaim at the paganism, and
Free-thinkers smile at the narrowness of it all. Of
course they are shocked and exclaim and smile. How
should they not?

Thus, in truth, a sojourn in Rome means an expan-
sion of view that is beyond words. Whereas up to that
time I had been accustomed to image Christianity to
myself as a delicate flower, divine because of its super-

natural fragility, now I saw that it was a tree in whose branches the fowls of the air, once the enemies of its tender growth, can lodge in security—divine since the wideness of its reach and the strength of its mighty roots can be accounted for by nothing else. Before I had thought of it as of a fine, sweet aroma, to be appreciated apart; now I saw that it was the leaven, hid in the heavy measures of the world, expressing itself in terms incalculably coarser than itself, until the whole is leavened.

So day after day the teaching went on. I was as a boy introduced for the first time to some great engine shed: the wheels roared round me; huge, remorseless movements went on; the noise and the power were bewildering; yet little by little the lesson was dinned into my head that here was something other than I had ever known, something I could never have learned in my quiet Northern twilight. Here were the business-offices of the spiritual world; here grace was dispensed, dogma defined, and provision made for souls across the world. Here God had taken His seat to rule His people, where once Domitian—*Dominus et Deus noster*—God's Ape, had ruled in His despite, yet shadowing God's Vicar.

On Good Friday, below the ruins of the Palatine, I stood in "S. Toto's" church and heard, " If thou let this Man go, thou art not Cæsar's friend." Now "This Man" is King and Cæsar is nothing. Here, indeed, if ever anywhere, has the leaven, plunged nineteen centuries ago by God's hand into the heaving soddenness of the Empire of Rome, gradually expressed itself in law and dogma under images of secular thought; here was the blood of Peter, that soaked into the ground below the obelisk, pulsing once more in the veins of Pius—*Pontifex Maximus et Pater Patrum*— scarcely a hundred yards away.

That at least I learned in Rome, and it was a lesson worth the conflict ten thousand times over. I had come out from a warm firelit room, full of shadows, into the shouting wind and great air spaces of human history. I understood at last that nothing human was alien to God, that the gropings of pre-Christian nations had brought them very near to the Gate of Truth; that their little systems and efforts and images had not been despised by Him who permitted them; and that "God, having spoken on divers occasions, and many ways, in times past, to the fathers by the prophets, last of all in these days hath spoken to us by His Son, Whom He hath appointed heir of all things, by Whom also He made the world; Who, being the splendour of His glory and the figure of His substance, and upholding all things by the word of His power, making purgation of sins, sitteth on the right Hand of the Majesty on high."

And if I learned that in Rome, I have learned once more in England that the Church of God is as tender as she is strong. She, like her Spouse and her type, His Mother, views all things, sees all men, controls giant forces; yet in her divinity does not despise "one of these little ones." To the world she is a Queen, rigid, arrogant, and imperious, robed in stiff gold and jewels, looking superbly out upon crime and revolt; but to her own children she is Mother even more than Queen. She fingers the hurts of her tiniest sons, listens to their infinitesimal sorrows, teaches them patiently their lessons, desires passionately that they should grow up as princes should. And, supremely above all, she knows how to speak to them of their Father and Lord, how to interpret His will to them, how to tell them the story of His exploits; she breathes into them something of her own love and reverence; she encourages them to be open and unafraid with both her and Him; she takes them apart by a secret way to introduce them to His presence.

All that I ever found in my old home, of guidance and rebuke and encouragement, I have found again at the hands of her priests, endowed, too, with knowledge as well as love. All the freedom of individual worship and thought that some think to be the glory of non-Catholic bodies I have found expressly secured to me in her temples, and have used it with far more confidence, since I know that her searching eye is upon me and that she will first call and at last strike swiftly if I wander too far.

Her arms are as open to those who would serve God in silence and seclusion as to those who "dance before Him with all their might." For, like Charity, of which she is the embodiment, she is patient, she is kind; . . . she beareth all things, believeth all things, hopeth all things, endureth all things; she never faileth. In her "we know in part, and we prophesy in part"; we are secure of what we have received, we are expectant of that which is yet to come. No one better than she recognizes that "we see now through a glass in an obscure manner," yet some day "face to face"; that now we "know in part, but then we shall know even as we are known." In her supremely I understand that "when I was a child I spoke as a child, I understood as a child, I thought as a child. But when I became a man, I put away the things of a child."

All, then, that is to be found in every other system, however eclectic, however adapted to the individual, is to be found here—all the mysticism of the North, the patience of the East, the joyful confidence of the South, and the fearless enterprise of the West. She understands and kindles the heart as well as she guides and informs the head. She alone holds up virginity as the most honourable state and matrimony as an indissoluble and holy Sacrament. She alone recognizes explicitly the vocation of the individual as perfectly as the ideals of the race; is reverent towards subjective faith as well as faithful to objective truth. She alone, in fact, is perfectly familiar and tender with the separate soul, understands its wants, supplies its deficiencies, deals carefully with its weaknesses and sins; simply because she is as wide as the world, as old as the ages, and as great-hearted as God.

As, then, I look back from this present moment, reading again the first page of these Confessions and sitting here in the house which once I visited years ago as a suspicious, timid, complacent boy, I see God's plan with me lying like a golden thread through all the tumbled country through which I have come, up from the pleasant meadows of home and school, the broken slopes of ministerial work, the caverns and cliffs of the shadow of death, up to this walled and battlemented plateau, from which for the first time the world is visible as it really is, not as I had thought it to be.

I understand now that there is coherence in all that God has made—that He has made of one blood all the nations of the earth; that there is not one aspiration out of the darkness that does not find its way to Him; not one broken or distorted system of thought that does not flash back at least one ray of eternal glory; not one soul but has her place in His economy. On the one side there is thirst and desire and restlessness; on the other, satisfaction and peace; there is no instinct but has its object, no pool but it reflects the sun, no spot of disfigured earth but has the sky above it. And through all this ruined wilderness He has brought me, of His infinite goodness, to that place where Jerusalem has descended from on high, which is the mother of us all; He has brought me out of the mire and clay and set my feet upon the rock; He has lifted me from those straying paths that lead nowhere, on to the broad road that leads to Him.

What yet lies beyond I do not know: the towers of this City of God rise immediately into the clouds that are about His Throne; the City is too vast, its streets too glorious, its houses too stupendous for any soul to dream that she knows them all or understands their secret. In this world, at least, not even the saint or the theologian, or the old man who has lived all his days within her walls, can dare to think that he has advanced more than a few steps within her heavenly gates. He stands within her, and, thank God, I stand there with him, as does every soul to whom God has shown this great mercy.

But all of us together are but a party of children wandering in from the country, travel-stained, tired, and bewildered with glory. About us are the great palaces, where the princes dwell; behind us that gate of pearl which, somehow, we have passed; the streets before us are crowded with heavenly forms too bright to look upon; and supremely high above us rises that great curtained stair way that leads to the King.

It is there that we must go presently, after a few more steps across the market square. Yet there is nothing to fear for those who stand where we stand; there are no precipices to be climbed any more and no torrents to be crossed; God has made all easy for those He has admitted through the Gate of Heaven that He has built upon the earth; the very River of Death itself is no more than a dwindled stream, bridged and protected on every side; the shadow of death is little more than twilight for those who look on it in the light of the Lamb.

"Behold, the tabernacle of God with men; and He will dwell with them... and God shall wipe away all tears from their eyes, and death shall be no more . . . And the City needeth not sun or moon to shine in it; for the glory of God hath enlightened it, and the Lamb is the lamp thereof."

ALSO FROM THE FISHER PRESS
THE PEARL OF GREAT PRICE
BECOMING A CATHOLIC- A PRACTICAL GUIDE
ANTONY MATTHEW

As the celebrations of the second millennium since the Birth of Christ draw nearer, the great Catholic tradition of Christendom is coming under closer scrutiny. Pope John-Paul II sees this as a time for the re-evangelisation of Europe. Antony Matthew believes that many fellow Britons have moments in their lives when they feel drawn towards this tradition. But they fail to take the necessary steps to become part of the Church to which many of their ancestors belonged. Often this is through ignorance of how to go about it, and a fear of the unknown. As a former Anglican, Matthew has already trodden this path himself, and so is able to give a first-hand account of what is involved in embracing the Faith, which has proved so resilient in Eastern Europe, and to which so many Europeans owe allegiance.

Pearl of Great Price is not a theological work. Its aim is to help people identify the grace of a call from God; and to provide practical advice on what they need to do to be received into the Church, and to live as Catholics today. Matthew presents an orthodox view: he deals with such issues as obtaining advice on the Faith, the process of religious change, handling family difficulties, parish life, the rhythm of the Church year, the liturgy, ways of preserving one's Faith, and living the Christian virtues.

He also covers Christian marriage, family life, Christian friendship and apostolate; and he shows how joining the Church can increase understanding and joy in Her two thousand year-long cultural tradition. Early chapters will be of most interest to those not yet within the Church. Those who are already Catholics will be encouraged by his later chapters to deepen their study of Her spiritual riches, and to act on his suggestions for strengthening their Faith, and handing it on to others.

The book is charmingly illustrated with line drawings by Mary Tyler, some showing the houses of British families which have remained Catholic over the centuries.

129x198mm   176 pages   ISBN: 1 874037 01 9
woodfree paper   £5.95

If you have difficulty in obtaining Fisher Press books from your local bookshop, you can obtain these direct from Fisher Press, Post Office Box 41, Sevenoaks, Kent TN13 6YN, England.